A TIME

OF

SECRETS

A TIME

OF

SECRETS

MIKE BOWEN

First published in 2004
by Pie in the Sky Publishing
PO Box 808
Armadale
Victoria 3143 Australia

National Library of Australia
  Cataloguing-in-Publication Data:

    Bowen, Mike.

    A time of secrets.

    ISBN 0 9752078 0 6.

    1. Bowen, Mike. 2. Irish – Australia – Biography.

    I. Title.

920.71

Original setting and editing from author's long hand – Tara Leonard
Cover and text design by Andrew Cunningham – Studio Pazzo
Typesetting and layout by Andrew Cunningham – Studio Pazzo
Printed in Australia by BPA Print Group

Author's note
The names of some of the people in this book have been changed
but the story remains the same.

DEDICATION

*To my Aunt Mary
everyone needs an angel*

CONTENTS

ACKNOWLEDGEMENTS

NO ONE CAN possibly climb Mount Everest on one's own. It takes a dedicated and committed team of people and I'm merely one of the team members. *A Time of Secrets* was only possible because of those magic people around me.

Firstly, I dedicate this book to my Aunt Mary—my own angel on earth—who unknowingly was my life's expedition leader and throughout offered me encouragement and showed unshakeable belief in my abilities when nobody else did.

Marie, the inspiration of my life without whom I would never have picked up a pen to write. *In hobbok.*

My sons, Jonathan and Emmett, for their constant encouragement and understanding. My ever close and constant companions.

Helen, their mum, who brought peace and purpose into my life when I needed it most.

Breda, my sister, for her continuous blessings, her love, understanding and kind consideration as to why I had to write such an open-hearted and frank account of our young lives.

Serica, for the joy of love she opened up inside me.

Marion, for the time of tranquillity, love and friendship she showed me.

Alan Sherratt, my business partner, confidante and friend, who has encouraged and supported me and who I hope will be by my side eternally.

Stef, the one who gave me his friendship and the confidence to become a good salesman.

Judie and Ray Belskie, in the glorious Barossa Valley in South Australia, for letting me use their beautiful home, *Blickinstal*, to write about this period of time.

Mike McMillan, Richard Froggatt and Austrian/Lauda Airlines who were enormously helpful and generous considering I have spent hours and hours on many trips over to and back from Ireland writing in the sky.

The late David Lean, for his beautiful movie, *Ryan's Daughter*, which lit the fire of inspiration in my soul. Some of this book was actually written in the now-dilapidated and Atlantic-swept original schoolhouse from the film. To this day, it sits overlooking the sea in the magnificent Slay Head Dun Chaoin area of the Dingle Peninsula, County Kerry.

Philip Colman, the hottest legal eagle in Australia, for his friendship and for allowing me the honour of rubbing shoulders with the legal fraternity.

Richard Rudski, for his guidance and thorough knowledge of the book world—a partner on whom I constantly rely.

Frank Peters, for his journalistic insight and outstanding contribution to the editing.

Thanks also to the production team that helped to craft the story into a book. In particular Tara Leonard who made a laborious task a joyful experience.

And, of course, my account of this passage of time could not have been but for the people who crossed my path and by whom I was lucky enough to be loved. The sad parts of my life add colour, for if everything in life was grey it would be boring and no one would be interested! So for the sad times I am also grateful for I have learned

ACKNOWLEDGEMENTS

a lot from them and am a better person as a result. And when you put it all together, the combined experiences of life have made me who I am. Liza's son.

Thank you, Ireland, for giving me the strength.

Thank you, Australia, for giving me the opportunity.

Mike Bowen

PREFACE

GROWING UP IN Ireland after World War II was a cold and hungry time for a lot of families and I'm sure ours was only one of many that struggled to stay warm and fed. Yet there was a strange sense of security about growing up in poverty. I suppose it's the old saying that you never miss what you never had and I can assure you our family missed nothing, considering we had nothing to begin with. Prejudice, discrimination and lies was the order of the day in the adult world, but among us young kids it was a different stage that we danced on. We didn't have a lot. But then again we didn't need a lot.

Ireland was immersed in a haze of deception and infidelity: what you saw was most certainly not what you got. It was a time of secrets, everyone had something to hide and I was no exception. Even as a child if you asked a 'difficult' question of your parents, you got a slap in the mouth and were told to go out in the sunshine while it was still there and God help you if you persisted in your line of questioning. But you wouldn't dare for fear of additional clouting. What was wrong?

Well, let's address one case and try to answer at least some of the problems that were there in my time, and who better a subject than this writer? I have been both disadvantaged and yet blessed to have come through that period. I am prepared to put my cards on the table, warts and all, and let he who is not guilty cast the first stone. This book is more an observation of a journey through a time in my life rather than a story, it is not intended in any way to criticise Ireland or its people. Rather, it is an attempt to understand why those things happened and what we can learn from them to help our children live a more open, honest life. Let's be brave and break the cycle of lies, for if we can't create a history of honesty and truth, how can we inspire our children?

For instance, one of the greatest deceptions is we send our children to war to create a better future. Lies, lies, lies! We send our children to war with our prejudices to protect our fears. If we were honest adults we would go to war ourselves and leave our children at home. What future do they have returning home to us in body bags or wheelchairs? One of the gifts I was given growing up in Ireland, was the strength to call a spade a spade and not a fork. I fear for our children if we are not going to be truthful with them and, really, whom better can they learn from if not their parents? No greater gift in life is given to a human being than the trust of God to raise and nourish a child, for if we can't be trusted with this most precious gift what else can we be trusted with?

I've been on a journey to hell and back and have also been the luckiest guy on this earth (though some people say you make your own luck). As a child I could not begin to imagine what it would be like to be held in my mother's or father's arms and to be told that they loved me and were proud of me. I've rubbed shoulders with the elite and I can swear to my God nothing comes close to being told by your mum and dad that they love you and that they are proud. It can never be said often enough. How life might have been different for me if I'd heard it only once, and maybe it became one of my demons because I just wanted to be loved and I desperately wanted to love someone like I had never been loved. But, sadly, I had virtually no tools of the trade, and the ones I had were badly blunted.

How could I bring a true and meaningful love to a relationship

after having none? No one showed me how to love. My sister Breda—
herself abused as a child—comforted me and taught me to survive.
Love to me (other than Aunt Mary's loving encouragement) was holding Breda's hand as she walked me from Gurranabraher through the
cold, snowy slush to the City Hall for regular health checks. Little did
I know she was going through her own hell, and what a hell that was.
But it was a time of secrets.

Ireland has seen its fair share of prodigal sons and I am only one
more. Hopefully by letting you look through my window you will see
a light in there that you can carry in your own heart and use to inspire
others. For I have learned to recognise and to learn from my demons
and I hope the same for you. Most importantly, don't be afraid to
love—regardless of the circumstances and heartaches—for it is better to have loved and lost than never to have known love at all.

And when all is said and done, I'm still just Liza's son.

Mike Bowen
Lauda Flight 09-2001 Vienna to KL
June 5, 2003

CHAPTER ONE

THE UNIVERSITY
OF LIFE

IT WAS MARCH 1973 and I had just arrived back in Dublin after a sales trip to England. There I was feeling on top of the world, a young man full of enthusiasm, looking forward to the following week when I would do my regular sales canvassing rounds in my beloved Kerry. Strange how Kerry had such a tight grip on me ever since I first crossed over its border some years ago. I had a feeling the first moment I put my foot on Kerry soil that it was going to affect my life in no small way.

I said farewell to my boss, Des, as I rushed to the railway station to catch the train on the last leg of my trip home to Cork.

I rode the train home full of excitement at the thought of seeing the children, Niall and Liz, but totally fed up with the thought of facing another domestic argument with Mary. Niall was four years old and a wonderful child: perfect manners, a beautiful smile and most affec-tionate. Liz was going on one: cheerful, playful and more like her mum than me. Two wonderful well-adjusted children—I think it's called a 'pigeon pair'. In my six years of marriage to Mary I never remember a day together when we did not have an argument. That was why I was spending nearly all of my time away from home. I was using every excuse I could think of to stay away from Mary because I was scared of the effect the fighting would have on the children. For I had already experienced that horror myself as a child, and I had sworn that I would not allow the same thing to happen to my children.

My thoughts were interrupted as the train stopped at The Corrougha station to drop off and pick up some more passengers. In a matter of minutes we were on our way again.

It was obvious from the conversation of the couple facing me that they had had a successful day's punting at Ireland's most famous racetrack (also called The Corrougha). As I listened to them, I began to think about how different our lifestyles were.

You see, I was born in Wolfe Tone Street just off Cathedral Road on the north side of Cork in a one room flat to Liza and Mick. Mick, being a docker and a very heavy drinker, decided a barrel of Guinness should be brought to the house and all his docker pals were invited to celebrate my arrival. Mick, in his younger day, was quite a good athlete and an excellent goalkeeper. He played for the local Freebooters side and carved his name in history in the Mardyke (soccer grounds) in a cup game against Shelbourne. Some say he could pick a ball off the ground with one hand as his hands were like shovels.

The offers flooded in to play with Belfast Celtic (now defunct), Glasgow Celtic, and Everton to name a few but no, Mick declined all offers. Freebooters, an amateur club, was paying Mick a handsome amount under the table and, of course, none of that money reached my mother Liza's hands to buy food or clothing. Occasionally he would come home and hand Liza two pounds ten shillings from his working week and then demand ten shillings back for a few drinks the next day. His drinking was a constant embarrassment to my only sister Breda and I.

I know Mick never set out to become an alcoholic and I never blamed him or was angry or ever disrespected him because of it. I'm not seeking martyrdom because of his problem, I'm just saddened of a childhood that could have been full of fun and sharing.

I often used to wonder why he ever married Liza. He was dark-haired, well-built and handsome, she was blonde and beautiful—everything in appearance—but they fought like cat and dog as long as I could remember. Of course, I now know why he married her: Liza was three months pregnant.

Liza was always in ill health, spending long periods of time in sanatoriums. She had tuberculosis and, in her absences, Breda and I were left to fend for ourselves because Mick would be unable to come home due to his drunken state on many a night. Breda and I were two lost souls: no money, no food, no heat and an army-issued over-coat full of fleas for bedclothes. Ireland in winter can be cruel to those impoverished; no wonder I constantly got bronchitis and pneumonia.

When Liza was not in hospital she would sometimes take me with her to the St Vincent de Paul's looking for food vouchers and then on to the other charities. No place was too humble for her except begging on the streets or asking her family for help.

My relationship with the nuns started when I turned four years old. Liza took me to the North Presentation Convent to start my schooling. We were both in a flood of tears for different reasons. Liza was crying becasue it was my first day at school and me because I was petrified of the nuns. The first thing I noticed about them was the leather strap that hung down from the waist, instantly registering dis-cipline in my mind and striking terror into my heart. However, first impressions can be wrong, as I was to find out. They were courteous and kind to me on many occasions. When Liza was in hospital they fed Breda and I, and gave us money to buy food for ourselves. I'm sure others who went to school at the North Pres Convent, as it was called, may not have been treated in the same manner as Breda and I were. I now know some of the nuns were less than kind to others than they were to us.

I was able to tap into their web of connections in later years when I became a rep, travelling throughout the country. They had a wonderful network amongst themselves and I was privileged to have access to it and them. They were a wealth of knowledge and influence, and they had money. On many occasions I would relieve them of the latter in the form of subscriptions for the organisation I represented and sometimes they would recommend me to their local parish priest or bishop whom I would also relieve of similar subscriptions, which was not very hard work for me at all. And, of course, I got a lot of the internal gossip—yes, nuns gossip too, as for that matter, do the priests. No doubt I could write a collection of books on their stories alone, but a dog doesn't bite the hand that feeds it now does it? Later, I realised that I had joined the society of silent conspirators for not speaking out. I suppose I too could be called a Judas, for as long as I was getting fed and receiving subs from them, my lips were sealed.

One didn't have to be an Einstein to figure out that some nuns had babies and priests lived with their housemaids and some nuns were lesbian and some priests were gay. It was common knowledge in religious circles and I had a key to the door, thanks to the relationship I struck up with the nuns in the North Presentation as a fumbling four year old. Little did I know what lay ahead for me and the relationship we would have for years to come, but the secrets I was privy to shall remain just that, for some nuns had strange habits in that time of secrets.

As a child in the 1950s, I soon learned the survival methods from Liza, as did Breda. I remember Breda and I doing the rounds of the convents looking for food. We told the nuns our mother was in hospital, our father was in England and our grandmother had just died, that there was no one to look after us and we were hungry. The nuns brought us in and fed us, then one of the nuns said, 'Didn't your nan die last month?' and quick as a flash I replied, 'That was my dad's mum, this was my mum's mum.' The nun said, 'You children are really getting a bad time. Look, here's five shillings, it will keep you going for a while. Oh, and by the way, you don't have a third nan do you?'

Liza was an excellent, discreet beggar and Breda and I learned the trade well. We had to, to survive. Of course, there were times when we didn't eat for days and then we would have to steal, but only what we needed, mainly milk and bread. And it was only a matter of time before that lifestyle started to affect us badly in our health.

Until we moved to St. Anthony's Road in Gurranabraher, we only ever lived in an absolutely atrocious, rat-infested single-room accommodation that was constantly damp and stinking. It certainly didn't deserve the title 'accommodation', I have seen animals live in better conditions. After moving on from Wolfe Tone Street and the equally bad situation of number 50 Shandon Street, 23 St. Anthony's Road was the next best thing to Buckingham Palace in our minds. It had a non-leaking roof and a toilet that we didn't have to share with four other families. So what if it was an outside toilet with a three-quarter door that let the rain and snow in during winter?

Our next-door neighbours at number 21 were Theresa and Christy Brew and their only child, Michael. Theresa was from Abbyleix in County Leish and, sadly, she was exploited as a girl; a victim of the Magdalene Sisters who enslaved young women in laundry work-houses in the name of Jesus Christ. This she told Liza, Breda and I on the second day we were at number 23. I remember Liza's face: a flood of tears as Theresa described her ordeals in detail to us. (I couldn't understand why Liza was crying as those things didn't hap-pen to her—such is the mind of a young boy.) In spite of it being a time of secrets lots of people knew what was happening in those institutions and no one did anything to save those young girls.

Liza and Theresa soon became friends and Theresa was a real char-acter and a woman with a big heart, a wonderful person. Christy, her husband, was a man who mostly kept to himself. Michael and I soon became friends, as children do, even though he was older than me.

The Davises were the neighbours on the other side: a refined, quiet, childless couple who were wonderful gardeners. Most of the other neighbours were kind to us and in no time they became like an extended family. Being a good Catholic street with no Pill or contraceptives available, there were lots of kids to play with, so who needed toys when you had friends?

Even though your friends were friends, it didn't stop them from giving you a roasting every now and again, so every time Mick staggered home drunk from the pub, singing as loud as he could, the lads would gave him a razzing and, of course, I would cop it the next day. It was very hurtful and embarrassing as the other lads' fathers didn't seem to like Guinness as much as mine, so I never got to giving them a roasting in return. It must be said, however, that when Liza would have one of her regular stints in hospital and Mick didn't come home, or was unable to make it home because of his drinking, we two poor souls were often fed by one of the other families in St. Anthony's Road.

Sometimes when Mick didn't come home Breda and I looked at it as a blessing for at least we didn't have to endure his drunken carrying on and singing Mario Lanza songs all the way home from the pub. Not that Mick wasn't a good singer, because he was, except he only ever sang when he was drunk. So the nights he wouldn't come home Breda and I would cuddle up together in my bed to keep ourselves warm from the bitter Irish cold, covered by the old army overcoats. And yet no matter what, being cold in St. Anthony's Road didn't ever feel as bad as being cold in Wolfe Tone Street or 50 Shandon Street. Strange logic isn't it?

There was no shortage of imagination in our street and as adolescents we turned to sport to occupy our over-active minds. Because no one had a real football in St. Anthony's Road, some of us lads would go down to the local abattoir at the end of McSweeney's Villas and get a still-hot bladder from a recently slaughtered animal and stuff it with newspapers to use as a football. It was really fun. Sometimes we would end up with as many as 20 players a side. We might start off with five a side, say, at 6.00 pm and as other mostly older lads were going to the movies or to meet their girlfriends they would join in the game for a while. Then some would leave and some would go home for a meal and afterwards come back to join in again so there would be a constant change in the amount of lads playing at any one time. The game sometimes went on for three hours.

Remember, there was no television to keep you indoors and what a wonderful way to meet lads from other streets. Your first encounter could be, 'Oh, fuck, my suit's ruined. My mother will kill me. This has got to go back to the pawn shop tomorrow.' Or, 'Hi, does your sister shag?' Yeah, Hollywood hasn't produced anything yet that I've seen to rival our suburb, Gurranabraher. Even blockbusters couldn't rival real life in Gurran—not in a million years.

The down side of living in Gurranabraher was having to lie when I applied for jobs when I was older. There was no way I could state that I lived in Gurranabraher for if I did the application would be ignored or rejected on the grounds of 'no vacancies at this time'. So my address was 23 St. Anthony's Road off Blarney Street. Discrimination against the poorer suburbs in Cork was rife. Of course, I vented my anger and frustration at some of the job interviews I attended but always to no avail. Sadly, influence and pull from other suburbs carried more than qualifications by someone from Gurran. But I can assure you it was all for one and one for all up in Gurran.

We had our fair share of strange and colourful characters . . . Tongie had a box cart. He was the local turf delivery boy, and anything else he could fit in to make an extra shilling. Seanie Mullins collected the food scraps from all the local households for the pigs. If he was relying on getting any scraps from the Bowen household his pigs wouldn't have survived long! Josa was an ex-Irish Guard who later in life had to settle for telling stories with the comfort of a pint in hand. Connie Baulty was a docker who worked with my father and who was quoted on many occasions for such jumbled stammers as, 'It's a disgrace there's plenty of idle ships walking around town and good men tied up at the docks.' Wacker Kenan was the local heavy or 'teddy boy', as they were then called. I remember one evening on my way home on the bus, he stood up at the back, brandishing a small axe and declared, 'I'm the top man around here and anyone who says I'm not gets this!' No one argued.

Nora the donkey got her name because she used to drive a donkey and cart. Billy the Bee wasn't a local, he was what you'd call a blow-in. Billy was treated as one of us because he was dating one of the women in our road, so he copped the usual flack that we graciously gave all the local characters, except Billy copped more because he was on crutches. Usually when he had a few drinks too many, us young rascals from St. Anthony's Road (Eugene Buckley, Willy Stack, Barry Cotter, Niall O'Keeffe, Pat Hurley, John Allen, Jimmy Mahoney and yours truly being the main core) were drawn to Billy like a moth to a flame. The poor sod surely has a place in heaven after the tough time he copped from us idle-minded lads—behaviour that I'm not proud of now.

We were told almost nothing by our parents and that made us a curious bunch, so when Willy Stack said he and an older boy from school had organised to take two girls up to the local woods in Sunday's Well, we all had to go along to see what was going to happen and hopefully queue up for a look. Maybe with a bit of luck, if the girls cooperated we also would get a try, except us younger ones didn't know what we were trying. The plan went well until it came to my turn and the girls decided they had had as much as they wanted. There I stood like a deserted bride at the altar until one of the girls took pity on me and said, 'You can have a feel.' Except I didn't know what to feel and when she guided my hand into her knickers I nearly died of fright when I touched her pubic hair. I thought she had a ferret or a mouse in there. The lads were in hysterics watching on. I quickly withdrew my hand and when I was later informed I would have had to put my penis into that, oh my God, I was glad I didn't get to be further up the queue earlier in the piece!

Masturbation came to a few of us in the strangest way. One day, a few of us saw Willy playing fetch with a dog. When he patted the dog as a reward for retrieving the stick the dog got frisky and started rubbing his penis on Willy's shoes. After many attempts the dog was not taking no for an answer so Willy proceeded to masturbate the dog to our bemusement. After a few tugs, Willy would walk away and the dog would follow. He would do this many times to frustrate the dog until the poor animal was going out of his mind (if he had one) and, of course, the rest of the lads and myself were in convulsions of laughter, rolling around on the floor.

Eugene Buckley and I were by far the most curious and adventurous. We would travel to Waterford, Limerick or Dublin at the drop of a hat, usually with no money in our pockets or, if any, rarely more than two bob. I don't remember ever buying a rail ticket. We would pick up a used one and if caught would lie our way out. We mainly travelled to see the soccer, so we would go to all the Irish international games and, of course, Cork, our local soccer team. We didn't do the rugby thing because it was much harder to get into those games for nothing. Not that we didn't like it, because we did, we just couldn't afford to go to the games.

Eugene shared his love for aircraft with me. On many occasions we would skip school and walk from home to the old Cork Airport (then called Farmers Cross) to see the planes. On one occasion we travelled to Dublin to see what we called real planes, the ones that carried more than two or four passengers. Dublin Airport was in its infancy then, without security, so Eugene and yours truly just walked out onto the tarmac, up the steps and sat in the pilot's and co-pilot's seats. After satisfying our young curious minds we then headed back to Cork. Now it's called 'hands-on education' and no, we never did any vandalising nor could we understand why others did. We would only take food when we were hungry or milk and lemonade when we were thirsty.

Yes, Gurranabraher was a wonderful place for a young fertile mind. Gurranabraher gave me my foundation, it gave me my strength. There, I learned to become streetwise among my peers who taught it to me better than any university professor. I learned dignity and respect from those around me and I also learned there was much that was kept from me.

Sure, I had aunts and uncles and two nans, but the attitude to Liza from Mick's family was, 'You're a bad housemaker and you had a good catch,' and the attitude from her family (with the exception of my darling Aunt Mary) was, 'You made your bed, now you lie in it.'

It's difficult for a child to walk tall when you have to carry the stigma of all that. However, the challenge was thrown to me at a very young age. I could either treat it as a millstone around my neck or as a stepping stone to the future. I had just started at the University of Life, and books were not required, but being streetwise was high on the list, so was survival. It was the perfect backdrop for anyone going into sales and, guess what I did? But until then I would only be known as Liza's son.

In spite of everything, deep down in my soul I believed I was destined for better things. I also believed if I was to fulfil my expectations, the piper would have to be paid many times if not in money then in pain for I learned that nothing comes to those without a price. And when all else failed, my driving force would always be there in the form of Aunt Mary's belief in me. 'Mike, son, you show them. You go out there and make a name for yourself. You may have been born in shit but you don't have to live in it. You are a wonderful young man.' Those words were like putting a tank full of petrol in a motorcar to a young kid like me. She was a reservoir of optimism and support, a terrific soul of a person.

She was a single mother too, but it wasn't what you're thinking. The story goes that her husband of less than twelve months, Mickey O'Connell (a fanatical greyhound man), died in mysterious circumstances. No one spoke of it. All of us young children were never told anything. We were given to understand that her daughter, Eva, was her natural child. I heard a different story years later that Eva was adopted from a woman in Glanmire and that she was born of parents in Dublin. Eva was tall and elegant and very pale-faced. She had an uncanny resemblance to my mother, but as I said, it was a time of secrets in Ireland.

※　　※　　※

I wished I could swap places with that couple on the train. I wanted their life but I couldn't imagine them wanting mine. Staring at my reflection in the carriage window and looking back over my life, I could understand why no one would be exactly queuing up to jump into my shoes. I decided enough reminiscing, no point in depressing myself any more. I had made up my mind while in England that I had to do something about my future.

A couple of toots of the train whistle let us know we had reached our destination. I collected my bags and struggled to my car. I was over-tired as I had not slept on the night boat. Once again I felt the fear shivers run up and down my spine. *God*, I thought, *there has to be a better reason for my presence on earth than to have to live in this sham of a marriage.* I started the car and instead of going home I headed for the Cotton Ball. This was one of the brighter bars in town, always full of gaiety, which was what I needed to give me courage to face going home. I was fighting fear and tiredness, hopefully a few drinks would make me forget both.

No sooner was I in the door than I saw a familiar face.

'Hi Mike, what are you having?'

Joe Rice and I had known each other for about four years. Joe knew just about every loose married woman that ever lived. No need for anyone who knew Joe to go without a good time.

'I'll have a pint of Double Diamond.' No sooner I had I taken the glass from my mouth than Joe's questions bombarded me.

'How was the trip? Did you get a shag? I bet you did, tell me about it.'

Joe was not interested in the success of my sales mission, he only wanted to know if I got a lay and did I have a name to add to his list? I was not sure what was getting to me most, the effects of the beer or the lack of sleep, but I was sure feeling drowsy. Within minutes Joe had organised a bed for me only two minutes from the pub. And I can tell you after another four pints of Double Diamond and singing my heart out, a bed close by was just what I needed.

I left at the crack of dawn to head home. It was good to see the children again. Oh, how I had missed them, they felt good to cuddle. How I wished that feeling could stay with me all my life (and it does to this day). It felt like the world had stopped forever. Kiss kiss kiss kiss, the warmest feeling in the world.

'Shouldn't you have been home yesterday?' the voice shouted down the stairs at me.

'Yes. Now I have got to repack and leave in an hour, so if I have a quick wash and drop Niall to school on the way I should be on time for my first appointment.'

'You've got some neck,' the voice shouted again.

'Sorry, I don't have time to argue. I've got to go. You ready, son? Got your school bag? Liz, kiss for Dad? Mmmm, love you.'

Niall shouted from the car door, 'Hurry, Dad or I'll be late for school!'

OK, the wash will have to wait and I'll get my clothes dry-cleaned in Kerry. I looked back at the tears in Liz's eyes and they cut me open like a knife. That was my punishment for a marriage gone wrong. I would discover in years to come what real pain was in many forms, and how cruel life could be.

I reached the office by 9.45 am precisely, as I am a stickler for punctuality—always was and always will be. It is one of the golden rules of professionalism.

Checked the mail, nothing important. One last phone call.

'Hi, Stef. Tralee tonight. OK. See ya.'

'Jesus, Michael, what's the hurry? How did you do in England? When did you get back?'

'Tell you all tonight when I see you, OK? Got to go.'

Stef was the consummate salesman and he was my mentor, the brother I never had, my consoler, my sanity in the times I thought I couldn't cope. He was my teacher, my hero and my clown for no one had a better sense of humour than Stef. I can't remember him ever being angry or being rude, he was always the perfect one. Our friendship went back a long way. Stef was the first Protestant I ever spoke to. When I met Stef I set myself a task—I must convert him to Catholicism. I'm glad I never succeeded. He had such a way with women, he made Valentino look like a altar boy. Stef, my hero.

Chapter Two

On The Road

I KNEW EVERY milestone on the way to Tralee, my heart sang every inch of the way. Everything that lead in and out of Tralee I loved. Even the smell—you name it—I loved it. Tralee was the centre of my life. I just couldn't get enough of it. If I could have eaten the very bricks that held the houses together, I would have. Little did I know my obsession was only to get worse.

Earl of Desmond Hotel on my left and another couple of minutes and Horans Hotel would be on my right after I passed the graveyard with its Celtic Cross dedicated to fallen IRA members. Tralee is a very pro-IRA town, one of its most loyal in the south. I almost drove past Horans where I usually stayed. When they were full, I stayed in the Grand Hotel.

'Hi Maureen, *cun is ta to mo shan blath?*' which means 'How are you my old flower?'—a term of endearment that I always use with good female friends and receptionists.

'Is five or seven free?' Those were my usual rooms, my homes away from home.

'I'll just leave the bag, Maureen, and will be in the bar having a pint.'

'Double Diamond please, Jim.'

'How's it going, Michael? Haven't seen you for a couple of weeks. Where've you been?'

'Just got back from England.'

'Fuck sake, no. Did you go and see United?'

'Of course, but that's not the reason I went.'

'Jesus, I thought the only reason any decent Irishman went to England was to see Manchester United.'

'Nah, I was there on business.'

'Ah, fuck off o' that.'

'I was trying to raise some funds.'

Jim quickly interrupted. 'For the boys was it?'

'No, in this case for a legit reason, OK.'

'I bet you didn't get a fuckin' pint like that from them rotten bastards over there, did ya?'

'No, Jim, you pour the best pint in Ireland.' And that was all he wanted to hear.

'Who's playing tonight?'

'D.J. and the Kerry Blues.'

'Should be a big crowd then.'

'Fuckin' chockers, boy.'

'Room seven is free.'

'Thanks, Maureen. See you later, Jim.'

'OK, then.'

Finally got that long overdue shower, then someone was calling at the door.

'Mike, Mike, it's Tom Fullam. What the fuck you doin' here? Thought you were travelling up north this week.'

'Yeah, but I spoke to Stef this morning and he said he would be here so I'll go north next week instead.'

'Can I share your room?'

'Sure, why not?'

'Can't get a bloody room anywhere. Everything's full. Oh, I told

John Loyal you were certain to get in here so he could share as well.'

'Where are we going to put Stef?'

'Worry about that later. Let's go for a pint—the solution to everything in Ireland.'

Before we got our mouths to the pints, John and Stef arrived.

'Make that another pint of Guinness for Stef and a scotch for John, Jim.'

'Two secs and I'll be with you, lads.'

'How about we have another few after this and then we'll grab some supper?'

'That sounds good and then we'll really get into it, OK?'.

The chorus responded.

'Who's playing tonight?' Stef asked.

'D.J. and the Kerry Blues.'

Well, someone was going to get some arse tonight then. No guessing who it was going to be. Always Stef.

Lucky we didn't have to go outside the hotel complex to the dance-hall as it was a typical March night in Kerry: raining cats and dogs, utterly pissing down and freezing as well.

Horans served the best mixed grill you could find anywhere in Ireland: chops, steak, bacon, black & white pudding, egg, mushrooms, sausages, beans and chips, lashings of bread and butter, and all for only ten bob. No messing around with menus here, boy. There was only one choice and who was complaining? John said he couldn't finish his because of his ulcer. I told him he just wanted more room for scotch. Stef was like me: not a scrap left on his plate.

Tom was a more conservative eater, totally opposite to his drinking habits. As we were commercial travellers (travelling reps) we met about once a month on our work journeys, like stars colliding in the night. Ha—more like all hell breaking loose!

Being residents of the hotel we didn't have to pay for the dance. So in we went. Chockers was an understatement.

'Christ, Stef, you'd need a shoehorn to squeeze your way up to the bar.' So we drank rounds two at a time. Two vodka and oranges for Tom and me, and scotches for Stef and John.

'Plenty of chances here lads,' said Stef.

I knew John wasn't interested, he was just happy to have drinking buddies. But Stef, Tom and myself were like greyhounds out of the trap. I was on my way to the bar for my round of drinks when I saw a familiar face.

'Michael,' she said. (I've never heard my name sound so beautiful.)

'Hi, Serica. Would you like a drink? Oops, sorry. Are you on your own or with Dennis?'

'Yes and no. Yes, I'd love a drink and no, I'm not with Dennis.'

'Oh, I'm sorry. I thought you were engaged.'

'I was. But now I'm not.'

After spending what seemed like a lifetime fighting my way to the bar for a drink I was petrified I wouldn't find her again. I wasn't going to risk leaving her to approach the bar again so I held her hand tight. There she was, the most beautiful face in the world.

Slainte, we said as we sat close.

'He's here tonight you know, and I'm trying to avoid him. Would you take me home?' she asked.

What an opening line! I was stunned. If I'd prayed my whole life I couldn't have got a wish like that.

I had met Serica about six months prior on a double-date with Maureen Boris and Dennis. Dennis was Serica's regular. Maureen and I had dated a few times. Serica and Maureen worked together at the Sunbeam factory. I remember sitting in the bar of the Farranfore Airport totally oblivious to the conversation going on, just staring at Serica's face. Dennis and Maureen must have known I fell in love with Serica in an instant. All through the night I tried to hide it, and when we returned to Dennis's house for tea afterwards I ended up in the kitchen doing the washing up with her.

Dennis tried to impress me with his bragging, showing off all the trophies his father won in his profession as an undertaker. I'd heard and seen strange things in my life, but trophies for undertaking beats the biscuit!

As I drove Maureen home later, I could not think of anything but Serica. Not a word spoken in the still Kerry air. I never went out with Maureen again and I hadn't seen Serica till now.

'We broke up a month ago,' says she. 'I couldn't see myself married to an undertaker.' I wasn't going to disagree.

'Are you on your own tonight?' she asked.

Oh shit, I forgot my round of drinks for the lads.

'Yes, I am,' I said. No question of who was getting priority in my life. Anyway, the lads had an understanding: if any of us got a pick-up, the rest would look after themselves.

Serica and I just stared at one another as if we were transported to another place where nothing else existed but us. Those few moments would entrap me into a lifelong admiration and deep love, a love I had never experienced or would ever experience again.

I felt her moist lips on mine: so gentle, so soft, so everything. The spell was broken with, 'Would you like to dance?'

'Would I like to dance? You bet.'

I was good, real good. *Sweetheart,* I thought, *am I going to impress you. I'm going to make such an impact on you that if you ever dance with other guys you won't be able to stop yourself comparing them to me.*

Gilbert O'Sullivan gave us our first dance experience with 'Get Down', a real hot number at the time.

'Where did you learn to dance like that?'

My mother, Liza, told me, 'Son, if you don't get good looks you get lots of other talents.' And when it came to dancing, I had an abundance of talent.

That night I used my dancing as a spider would use his web to entrap a fly. But who was entrapping who? I was melting in her arms as Tony Orlando and Dawn sang 'Tie a Yellow Ribbon Round the Old Oak Tree'.

The soft touch of her waist, the smell of her hair, her beautiful Kerry accent. Then she said, 'Let's go, baby.' An old cliche, but boy did it sound good.

We smooched in the car outside her house in Mitchell's Avenue with Glen Campbell singing Jimmy Webb's beautifully crafted songs. I didn't care if the world ended then because I was in heaven anyway.

I began to think about all the times I had parked only a few yards further down the road with Maureen Boris who also lived in Mitchell's Avenue and all I could think of then was a score or, as we say in Cork, a shag (mind you, I never got one). Now all I wanted to do was to be held like a baby, gently. I had been with many women and it never felt like this. I was excited, scared, and confused all at once. My body felt like it was having a chemical explosion. I thought, *This is the definition of love.*

But wait a minute, you can't do this in Catholic Ireland, you can't be married and love someone else. You can flirt, you can shag, you can do almost anything else, but you can't fall in love. I was checkmated before I even made my first move. What was I to do? I thought of the old adage: when in a crisis don't do anything because it's always diffi-cult to make a logical decision in an illogical situation. *I will tell her the next time I see her,* I thought. This way I would have more time to pre-pare myself to tell her the truth.

Even though we were only together for a few hours, I had no doubt in my mind that it was the start of a forever. Where the path of life leads you can be a long way from the one you thought you were head-ing towards. How true this would prove for me.

'I've got to get some sleep,' Serica whispered. 'It's after three. Do you want to see me again?' she said, as if I might not.

'Of course.'

'When?'

'Tomorrow night, OK? I'll pick you up at 7.30.'

Glen Campbell's 'Where's the playground, Susie?' was playing as she waved to me and tiptoed down the pathway to her door.

Back at the hotel, I rummaged for spare pillows and blankets to sleep in the bath as Tom, Stef and John occupied the beds. There was no hope of waking the lads for they were all tanked up. Unusual for Stef—it must have been the first time he'd been to bed before me—but I wouldn't bet he missed out on a shag that night. I'd seen Stef operate at lightening speed.

As the lads headed off in their different directions after breakfast I agreed to meet with Stef for morning tea after I had returned from Myvane, a small town about 35 miles north of Tralee.

I jumped in the car nursing a sore head from a combination of drink and sleeping awkwardly in the bath. I chuckled to myself when I realised I had spent more time in the hotel's bath last night than I did in my entire youth. We didn't have a bath in our house when I was growing up, just a basin job was good enough for us.

Kerry looked even more beautiful as I drove to Myvane. I've always said if anyone dies on this earth without seeing Kerry then they haven't seen anything worthwhile. And if heaven doesn't look like Kerry, it's not worth going there. So, Lord, just leave me in my beloved Kerry.

I was back in Horans by 10.50 am waiting for Stef. Unlike me, he is almost always late. I remember waiting for him one day in Limerick for hours and when he finally arrived he greeted me with the usual, 'Hello, M-I-C-H-A-E-L, boy. What's new?' No point getting upset, that was Stef and he would never change. As he says in his Cork brogue, 'I may be late but I always turn up, don't I?'

I was to meet him at noon at The Wentworth Hotel in Limerick. I had drunk God knows how many pints by the time he arrived. 'What kept you?' I mumbled. He told me to go up to the foyer in the hotel and pick out the best looking bit of stuff and tell her she could now join us. Knowing Stef I didn't hesitate. The alcohol in my system soon stabilised when I saw her.

'Are you with Stef?'

'Yes. I'm Poppy.'

'I'm Michael.'

'I know,' she said. 'He described you perfectly.'

I felt flattered. 'Come and join us. What are you drinking?'

'Vodka,' she replied.

Stef already had a pint of Guinness in front of him. I was beginning to wonder where I was going to put any more pints. I ordered a vodka and orange for myself and a straight vodka for Poppy.

I asked Stef if we were going dancing. He said, 'Let's wait and see.' I was getting worried that I might have to act the raspberry or miss out on picking up a bit of skirt. Stef assured me all was in hand. 'Don't worry, you'll get a fla (a shag). I promise.'

It was 9.30 and still Stef was as cool as a cucumber. He smiled and said, 'Don't worry, b-o-y, you'll be alright.'

'Oh yeah, that's alright for you to say,' I groaned. 'You've got a ride for the night.' He gave me a big grin and I began to understand his meaning. *Fuck no, he can't be meaning we share. No, surely, no.*

'Finish that, my shout.' By now he was drinking single scotches and buying doubles for Poppy. I don't know what was holding me up but I was drinking myself sober. I was actually getting more coherent.

By 11 o'clock I had given up hope of going dancing. I told Stef I had forgotten to book a room for the night.

'Shit, what will we do?'

'Don't worry, boy,' was the reply, 'leave it to me,' he said as he casually approached the reception desk. I thought I would make a serious proposition to Poppy.

'Am I getting a shag?'

'You bet.'

Instant erection and a smile from ear to ear.

We were interrupted by an American accent: 'Hey, sweetheart, do you mind if we join you guys for a drink?' They had been watching us for some time hoping to cut in. The adrenaline rushed to my head.

'Fuck you, cunts,' I screamed as I cleared the table in front of me and grabbed a chair, swinging it wildly above my head. I wasn't having any smart-arse fucking Yanks taking my prize. I didn't give a shit how tough those bastards were. No one, I mean no one, was going to cut in on me. They both backed off quick—real quick.

'Listen, cunts, you guys been reading too many leprechaun stories. Well, this ain't no fairytale. Now get fucked.' And off they staggered.

Stef walked over to me clapping. 'Very good, boy. Very good. Fucking hell, boy, you looked like John Wayne there, all you were short of was your guns.'

'Piss off, Stef, where were you when I needed you?'

A real droll reply: 'Sure, you were doing alright, Michael, boy, without me. You were doing fine.'

The night porter arrived to dress me down over my conduct but after explaining my defence he just winked and said, 'Yankie bastards.' I slipped him a quid for his trouble.

Poppy excused herself to go to the toilet and in the same breath said, 'I'll see you in bed in a few minutes.' I told Stef to take his time in the bar and to give me at least a half hour start. I was up the elevator and into my room in record time. I stripped in bed waiting for Poppy to arrive. Ten minutes, no Poppy.

Fucking Yanks, I'll kill the rotten, bloody bastards.

I jumped out of bed, went down the lift and didn't realise until I was standing in front of Stef that I hadn't put my clothes back on.

'Who are you trying to impress?' he said.

'Oh, fuck,' I replied looking down.

'Nice one,' he smiled.

'Stef, them shit Yanks must've taken Poppy to another hotel.'

'No, boy, she went up in the lift about five minutes ago,' he answered.

In no time at all I was up in the lift and into bed again. Five minutes later and no Poppy so down the lift again in the nuddy.

'Jesus, Stef, I'm like a fuckin' yo-yo going up and down in that stupid lift. You know what, I think I could have an orgasm just going up and down in it without ever throwing my leg over Poppy. If I don't find her soon I think I will.'

Stef smiled at me.

'What now?' I pleaded. 'Where is she?' He assured me she went to my room. He saw her go into the lift. Finally I realised there were two lifts.

'That one,' he said, pointing to the other one. 'Shithead.'

I pressed the button and the door opened and, oops, sure enough, there was Poppy on the ground, drunk as a skunk, pissed as a maggot. Stef smiled a broad smile and said, 'Go get it, son.' I lifted her to her feet and struggled down the corridor to the room. 'Drunk or not Poppy, darling, you're coming to fulfil your promise.' And, boy-oh-boy, did she fulfil her promise. I learnt a lot of new tricks that night and Stef, true to his word, didn't let me down. Stef never let anyone down.

❀　　❀　　❀

'Hi Stef, late again.'

'How's it goin', Michael, boy?'

I ordered two cakes and two teas.

'How did it go last night?'

'Stef, I'm afraid,' I said.

'What's wrong?' he asked, concerned.

'I'm afraid. I've never felt like this before, and I can't explain … there isn't a word to explain how I feel.'

'You look alright to me, Michael, boy.'

'I'm sure I do, Stef, but I've got this knot in my stomach.'

'You probably feel that way because you didn't get a fla last night.'

'No, Stef. Nothing like that.'

'Who was she? Who did you shift last night?'

'Her name is Serica.'

'Serica,' he said crumpling his face. 'You mean the one you double-dated with Maureen Boris?'

'Yeah, that's her.'

Stef was getting excited. 'The one who's working in the Sunbeam? Oh, shit, isn't there a girl working there from Cork? What's her name, ah, let me think . . . oh, yeah, Theresa Feddis. Oh, for chrisakes, be careful, son.'

'Stef, I don't care. I think I'm in love.'

'Fuck off you stupid prick, don't be silly. Fla her, then leave her or maybe fla her a good couple of times because she's gorgeous and then leave her. For chrisakes all girls are like the Gurran bus: there's always plenty and there's always one due or another one around the corner.'

'Stef, Stef, listen I know all that, but this feels different.'

'Oh yeah, how?'

'I don't know, Stef, because I never felt this way before. I feel stupid. I feel like crying. I feel like laughing. The whole lot put together and it doesn't make sense. Stef, I don't know how many women I've had and I didn't give a shit, you know that.' Then the tears started to run down my face. 'Help me. I don't want to fall in love, I don't want trouble, but I can't help it. I just knew, Stef, the minute I saw her last night my heart stopped. It's a crazy feeling, a frightening feeling and a magic one all at the same time.'

Stef just looked at me and I knew I had his support. He never told me but I knew he loved me like a brother. We had a special bond.

'Mike,' he said, reaching across the table and patting my hand, 'Boy, just be careful.' Then he smiled and said, 'At least she's beautiful unlike some of your recent birds.'

We parted with, 'See you soon.'

Chapter Three

SERICA

BEEP-BEEP. I TOOTED outside her gate and she appeared. In a second my heart started to flutter. She looked divine. I thought to myself, *Am I the luckiest bugger on earth or what?* No question about it.

'Hi, Michael. Spot on time.'

I was having trouble trying to answer, so many thoughts were going through my head.

'You look delicious,' I said, and then felt foolish. I think no matter what I'd said I would have felt foolish anyway. She looked stunning and I just couldn't put it into appropriate words. She smiled and said, 'Ah, go way o' that.'

'Where to, madam?'

'Wherever you like.'

'How about Killarney? *Ryan's Daughter* is showing there.' No need to wait for an answer, the smile said it all.

The movie just knocked me for dead, everything about it, I was in heaven. I had no idea, as I sat through David Lean's love epic, of the web it was weaving around me.

Dun Chaoin in Slay Head and the schoolhouse in the movie were to make a big impact in thirteen years time, and further on into my life, but for now nothing in the world mattered. I was in love and I had Everything, with a capital E. How simple the world looks when you are in love, all else is trivial. It's like being suspended in animation. The ultimate high. Then utopia was broken when the storyline of the movie turned to sadness, and Ryan's daughter didn't get to live happily ever after with the love of her life.

Surely this couldn't happen in real life, after all, it's only a movie. I didn't really care because I was taking the love of my life home later that night and it was all that mattered to me. I was soaking up every minute of that blissful feeling—something I rarely experienced in my youth. I certainly didn't have that kind of feeling from Mary in my marriage. Now, I felt like a king. The boy from Gurranabraher with patches on the arse of his pants had come a long way.

Out on a date with the best-looking girl in the world, who could ask for anything more? All this was going through my head as I kissed her at every opportunity, and there were many. I hated taking her home after the movie, I wanted it to last forever. No, even forever would have been too short a time. I drove slowly back to Tralee through Farranfore. Every minute was precious and every minute with her was one that I wasn't alone.

We smooched and cuddled for another fifteen minutes or so in the car before she had to go.

'What are you doing Saturday?' she asked.

'Don't know,' I replied. 'Why?'

'Maureen Boris is getting married and all the girls from work are going. Would you like to come?'

'Hold on a sec, did you say Maureen Boris? I didn't even know she was going out with someone.'

'Oh, yeah,' she grinned, 'He's from the north.'

'Sure, I'd love to, but doesn't she have to invite me?'

'OK then, why don't you come to the reception afterwards, then that way they won't mind because most of them will be pissed. I'll see you around four at the reception venue,' were her parting words as she blew me a kiss. Saturday couldn't come soon enough.

I spent all of Saturday morning kissing and hugging Niall and Elizabeth trying to get rid of my feelings of guilt. I was choking on it for I knew it was only a matter of time before the family would break up. This loveless union was justifying my actions. How could I possibly reconcile, when I had no respect in my so-called marriage? Mary, the children and I lived with her parents with not an ounce of privacy in our lives, worse than living in a fish bowl.

I had thought once you got married, you got to live as a separate family and built your own future. Not in this case, definitely not. Mary wasn't leaving her mum and dad, and I would have to accept that. Strange how it had never been brought up before the wedding. Originally it was only going to be for a few months, but a few months had lasted six years and never looked like ending. I had desperately wanted to move into our own home and live what I thought would be a normal life. No way in the world would I have married Mary had she told me we were going to spend the rest of our lives with her parents.

The whole marriage ceremony was a disaster on the day. You don't have to wonder why: it was April the first. April Fool's Day—how appropriate. As expected, Mary was late to church and went berserk when the little flower girl tugged at her veil and it almost came off.

Then I walked into the changing room at the hotel only to see Mary's aunt who had brought her boyfriend from England for the wedding (and not her husband, mind you) having a good old shag on the bed. I was embarrassed but they certainly weren't. And then I discovered I had picked the wrong band for the reception. I had met previously with Peter Prendergast, who managed The Dixies Showband, and he told me he could get Rory Gallagher and The Impact Showband for a fiver and pompously I told him to get fucked. Little did I know the mistake, or should I say mistakes, I was making. How stupid was I? Rory goes on to become a world-class guitarist, with record sales in the millions, and my marriage ends in disaster. April first is definitely Fool's Day.

Then there was the issue of Mary's bed-wetting. Not occasionally, but every night, and there was no way she was going to discuss the matter with a doctor or with me. You can imagine how shocked I was on our honeymoon in our Dublin hotel.

It was my first time having sex and the same for her. First of all, I didn't like it and wondered what all the fuss was about. Then I thought I did the deed all wrong and, to make matters worse, I woke up soaking wet. I thought I must have shoved it in too far and stabbed her bladder or something. *Oh, shit, what did I do? How do we dry the mattress? What will the housemaid say in the morning? What the Christ am I going to tell me pals? Fuck, panic, don't know, don't know. Calm down. Calm down. Breathe slowly. Oh, fuck, if I do that I might die and if I don't die from panic the hotel manager is going to kill me anyway.* Mary just lay there utterly blasé. I stripped the bed at 2 am and did so every night for five nights, cutting our honeymoon short.

On our return, we discovered the aunt from England had been using the wedding bed with her boyfriend as a 'work bench' for the duration. I voiced my disapproval to Mary and on Sunday morning I left the house on my way to Mass with her shouting out the bedroom window, 'I hate you, you bastard.' And so my marriage was finished before it started.

That was the reason I started travelling work-wise: I couldn't get used to sleeping in a wet bed. There were a couple of times when I tried to stay at home for a period (hence Niall and Elizabeth), but I was beginning to feel enough time had passed—six years in fact—and there was no hope of me being the husband and father that I wanted to be.

In contrast, I was greeted with that stunning smile on arrival in

Tralee at 4 pm sharp. A black dress with white ribbon trim, about two inches above the knee, was wrapped around her perfect shape.

I coolly made my way to the dance floor in my faded purple jeans and purple jumper with a yellow horizontal stripe around the middle. I put my hands around her and kissed her passionately. The band was playing, 'Tie a Yellow Ribbon Round the Old Oak Tree'. She said, 'Can this be our song? It was playing the first night you took me home.' I just loved the idea. 'Because you travel so much, every time you come home to me, I can sing it for you and we can request it at a dances.'

'You got it,' I said in my Dick Bogarde voice.

Her eyes pierced my very soul. Then she stood on her toes to kiss me, so softly and yet so passionately. She whispered, 'I think I'm falling in love with you.' I whispered back, 'When will you know?' She just beamed at me with that killer smile. For every ounce of enjoyment I was absorbing I would pay for it dearly in the future, but that was yet to come. For now, Tralee was heaven-on-earth and I was like a two-year-old child in a sweet shop.

'Michael,' Marta Kyrnes shouted, 'Lads, what are you up to after this?'

Marta Kyrnes was the sister of Mary Kyrnes, whom I had dated a few times, come to think of it. Marta and I also went out a few times, usually dancing. She was a fab dancer and a bloody good drinker too. Great fun to be with. One night, Marta and I stopped everyone in the Brandon Hotel at a dance, while D.J. and the Kerry Blues played. We had the floor to ourselves as everyone just stared and gasped in admiration. Boy, did we put on a dancing display! She was good, and we were hot.

'Marta, I'm taking him to bed,' Serica said out of the blue, with a tantalising grin.

'I'll see you in The Brogue or The Abbey then tomorrow if you aren't too exhausted after your erotic night.'

We both shouted, 'See you Marta!'

The MC called for everyone to gather around to see off the newlyweds. We all gathered in a circle and the bride and groom made their way round to everyone. I shook hands with the groom and kissed the bride with far less enthusiasm than I ever had before. She winked and slid her eyes across to Serica as if to say, 'You look great together.' I don't propose to be a mind reader, but sometimes you know when actions speak louder than words.

As soon as the bride and groom left for the honeymoon Serica and I headed for Horans Hotel. I was booked into room seven again. I had never looked forward to anything so much in my life and in a flash I was carrying her over the threshold.

The purity of the passion we both felt and expressed can never be repeated or described in everyday language. I was higher than high and to even try to put it into words would be to try and put the experience into normal terms, and that it certainly was not. Nothing else in my life would ever give me a bigger high.

Oh, fuck, it's 3.30.

'Wake up Serica, your mother will kill you.' No staying out all night in Tralee or anywhere in the whole of the county, for that matter. If you were a female, you would cop the wagging tongue of your mother and the neighbours for things like that.

'Jesus, where's me dress?'

'I'm looking, I'm looking.'

'Oh, shit. It's got feathers all over it from the pillows.' We both laughed as I wiped the dress with a damp facecloth. And then in the panic came a moment of calm beauty. She caught my hand, pulled me close, kissed me and whispered, 'I hope I'm pregnant.' I couldn't reply. I was stunned. As if to reassure me she said, 'You know, you're the first. Dennis and I never did it. I wanted it to be with someone special and that's you.' I still couldn't answer, but the tears flowed. No woman had ever spoken to me like that before, with such sincerity and passion. My brain was telling me I couldn't cry (what about that macho thing!), but my heart was ignoring it. Logic doesn't come into the love thing, the heart takes over. Even with the wrinkled dress and hair, she looked a stunner.

'C'mon, that's everything. Let's get you back to your mother before I get into her bad books,' I said, wiping my eyes.

'It's ten past four so just be as quiet as you can going in, OK?'

'It doesn't matter how quiet I am, my mum won't go to sleep until I come home. But don't worry,' she answered, 'I'll tell her a bunch of us were drinking and having a criac at Horans after the wedding.' That comment slowed my heartbeat somewhat.

'Would you like to come to Mass with me in the morning?' she asked.

Wow, a date to go to Mass, how original.

'You bet. Noon Mass. I'll pick you up at 11.45.' She kissed me good-night and I waited until she disappeared through the door with her shoes in her hands.

I wrestled with my conscience for the remainder of the night. It was impossible to sleep. What would happen if someone told her I was married? What would she do? What would I do? Questions and counter-questions, answers that made no sense and, if they did, I couldn't do anything about it. It was impossible to clear my mind. I alternated between reading old soccer programs that I always brought with me and listening to Radio Luxembourg.

It seemed like an eternity till dawn, but as soon as it arrived, I drove down to St. John Church in Castle Street to buy the Sunday papers. They're sold outside almost every church in Ireland on Mass days: one Irish paper to check the local news and one English paper to check the soccer results. The first result almost every Irishman looked for was Manchester United. Up to now, United have had two Irishmen captain them: Johnny Carey and Noel Cantwell. (I'm sure that's the reason for the loyal Irish fans. Of course, another Irishman, Roy Keane, would captain them later on and find even greater success.)

Yes! United won 2–1 against Chelsea.

'Did United win?' from over my shoulder. Looking back with my paper in total disarray I saw Theresa. Holy shit, Theresa Feddis.

'Hi, Theresa. How are you?'

'Fine.'

'Yeah, they won 2–1.'

'What are you doing in Tralee on a Sunday morning?'

'I was at Maureen Boris's wedding yesterday.'

'So was I.'

'How come I didn't see you?'

'Don't know. I arrived at about four.'

'Oh, I had to leave at three. Were you on your own?'

'No, I was with Serica.'

'Serica,' she said, thinking.

'You know her, Serica Mc—,' . . . but before I could finish her name, she interrupted.

'I thought she was engaged to Dennis what's-his-name? Oh yeah, I remember now: Mary Kyrnes told me last week she broke up with him after about two years. We all thought she was going to marry him, you know.'

'How are you enjoying living in Tralee?' I enquired.

'Sure, I love it and who wouldn't love Tralee? But I go home to Cork every four weeks.'

I quivered when she said that, and I quivered even more when she asked me, 'Where do you live in Cork?' I quickly lied, 'Spur Cross.' She told me her family lived in Cathedral Road. I nearly shat myself when I heard that. My nan and cousins lived about five minutes from there. That's walking mind you, not driving.

The ground was getting softer under me or my knees were getting wobbly. Stef was right, I was going to have to keep as far away from Theresa Feddis as I could. Stories travel fast in Ireland.

'I've got to go,' I lied with a smile. 'See you round.'

After a hearty breakfast and reading my papers, it was time to pick

Serica up for our date. I don't remember ever feeling so excited about going to Mass before. It wouldn't have mattered to me if Mass was going to run all day as long as I was with Serica.

The sun was shining. It was a beautiful day.

At 11.45, I was tooting outside Serica's door. I couldn't wait to see her. I didn't want to knock on the door in case her mother killed me for bringing her home so late the previous night. The door opened and my worst fears were realised. Her mother beckoned me. First, I thought she wanted to kill me, then I thought that Serica might be sick and she wanted to tell me. I got out of the car, straightened my tie, put on a brave face and walked to the door.

She smiled and said, 'Serica isn't . . .'

My heart stopped beating.

'. . . ready yet. Would you like to come on in?'

My heart started up again. I was lost for words, 'Ah . . . ah . . . no, I'm fine. I'll wait here.'

Serica poked her head around the door, 'Come in, I'm just putting on my nylons.'

I was lost. I wasn't ready for a friendly mother. I was expecting a bollocking and I was confused. 'OK, Michael, I'm ready. Let's go.' This girl couldn't look bad even if she came out of a coalmine.

'Oh, by the way, Bishop Casey is saying Mass, and it's High Mass. You still want to go?' she asked.

'Yeah, yeah,' I said.

How ironic. When I now look back at the sermon that day about sex and infidelity, I think of all people who might throw stones and Bishop Casey should have been among the last. I'm sure he's suffering in his own hell now . . .

For those of you who don't know Bishop Casey, he was the Bishop of Kerry and later moved on to become Bishop of Galway, a man with a bubbling personality and a great sense of fun—certainly one of the highest profile people in Ireland. A charming man.

He pounded the pulpit that morning and told the congregation to abstain from sex unless you were married and intended to have children while doing the deed. If not, you were committing a mortal sin. And as he spoke those words I nearly swallowed my Adam's apple with guilt. Of course, years later we found out the good Bishop wasn't practising what he was preaching, and fathered a son to his American–Irish mistress, Annie Murphy. The news sent Ireland into shock.

The younger generation of Ireland viewed the good Bishop's indiscretion differently, they saw it as a liberation from the over-dominant Catholic Church. However, it was not uncommon to regularly hear some of the older people say, 'Oh, sure, wasn't it her fault? She seduced him and him a man of God.' Ireland was in denial and Bishop Casey moved to South America.

Of course, the moral of this tale is if you're Bishop of Kerry you can screw all you like but if you are a layperson in love you can't. Hindsight is a wonderful thing because if this information was available then, how different my life might have been.

Mass finished at one and it's almost religion in Ireland to go for a drink before dinner to work up an appetite.

'Where to, madam?'

'How about The Bridge Inn? Oh, and by the way, Mum said you're coming to dinner.'

'You're kidding.'

'I'm not.'

'Oh, shit no,' I smiled.

'Oh, shit yes,' she smiled cheekily.

'She wants to bollock me over last night, I bet.'

'No, she doesn't. She just wants to check you out to make sure you're good enough for me. She doesn't want me going out with any Tom, Dick or Harry, you know,' she teased.

After her three vodkas and my three pints I was ready to face my judgement, although not willing, because I was beginning to feel the pressure of hurting another person's feelings when the shit hit the fan. I lied my way through a lovely dinner and I was feeling awful guilty because I was beginning to like the woman. She was being so hospitable to me and seemed genuinely concerned that her daughter was going to be loved and respected by me.

I was humbled by the woman's concern and could only wish it was a different time in history and all would work out fine, but I knew in my heart of hearts that it was only a matter of time before it all blew up in my face. I wanted to tell them the truth, but I couldn't. I was scared. I loved her daughter. I didn't know any other way to handle the situation. I just loved Serica and I didn't want to lose her for anything. Every minute was precious and I would have done anything to hold onto her. I know it was selfish. I know it was wrong. I know it was stupid, but love was the strongest thing in my life then. Love felt like the only thing in my life.

'Mrs Mc—, I'm so grateful,' I was about to say when Serica said, 'She's Serica too, you know.' Serica senior nodded her head to confirm and I beamed.

Not a word was mentioned at dinner of Serica's dad or brother, as Serica previously told me her dad died some years ago and her brother lived away from home. She also had a sister, Nola, married and living in England with a daughter. And what else could you call a granddaughter but Serica? *Three in the family,* I was thinking. *Maybe luck comes in threes.* But again I was kidding myself, grabbing at straws. I was hopelessly in love—I suppose addicted is a more appropriate description.

Serica's mum insisted I sit and not help with the cleaning up after dinner in spite of my offering. Men in Ireland were not expected to help in those matters, it was classed as 'sissy'. I sat by the fire drinking a bottle of Phoenix beer as the two Sericas cleaned up and I felt giddy. I was not used to being fussed over.

Strange old world, isn't it? Just a few hours ago I thought Serica senior was ready to bite my head off and now here I sit getting the royal treatment. And I being the culprit of culprits deceiving both lovely human beings and having stolen Serica's virginity only last night.

I felt the tears about to flow when I caught Serica's concerned look. 'You OK, Michael?'

'Yeah, sure. I'm fine,' and I smiled. 'It must have been the late night,' I whispered. She wiggled her bum. 'Want to go for a spin?' she asked with a sly grin. 'Yep,' was my reply.

'Thank you Mrs Mc—. Dinner was beautiful.' I caught her by the hand and said, 'I love Serica.' She nodded and said, 'I know you do. Just be good to her, that's all I ask.'

I left with Serica, thinking how cruel a break some people are dealt for we'd all been dealt a shit hand. But there must be some reason for it, I just wished I knew what the outcome would be.

'Where to, tidy bum?' I asked her.

'Fenit,' she replied, sheepishly.

'Fenit it is.' I wouldn't have given a damn if she'd said the moon. For this lady I would be happy to drive round the world.

April in Ireland is not the best time of year to be suntanning on a beach in Fenit. But it was still beautiful sitting in the car cuddled up listening to Radio Luxembourg playing Slade's 'C'mon Feel the Noise', Gilbert O'Sullivan's 'Get Down', and Don McLean's beautiful tear-jerker 'Vincent'. This is how memories are created, as we sat in a Ford Escort on a bleak Sunday afternoon with the sun afraid to come out from behind the clouds, curled up in the back seat looking out on the beautiful Bay of Tralee.

What a shame, I was thinking, *that we can't stop the clock.* Someone told me once: you can't appreciate the good times unless you've experienced the bad ones. I'd had lots of bad ones, that was why I was on such a high

'Michael, I meant what I said last night, about being pregnant. I love you. I really do.'

Fear ran up my spine. *What should I say?* Was now a good time to drop my bombshell? I couldn't think fast enough. *Why spoil a beautiful day? I'll tell her next time.* I was in a panic.

'Do you love me, Michael?'

'Serica, I can honestly say I've never loved anyone, ever, like I love you. I'm overwhelmed by you, honest I am.'

'Michael, will you marry me one day?'

'Serica, I could not think of anything more I would want in life. I will always love you no matter what happens and don't you ever forget it. What's happening here is something special and one day I'll write about it and then and only then will you understand the extent of my love for you.'

'Ah, go away o' that,' she said, 'You're making me blush.' We kissed passionately and then agreed to go for tea, a quick stop at The Abbey for a pint of Double Diamond and a vodka. Then dinner at Cordon Bleu in the square: a mushroom omlette for me and a plain one for the lady and, of course, lots of chips and bread and tea . . . and the bill for three pounds, four shillings and two-pence.

Smiles and an abundance of small talk kept us busy until it was time to join the Sunbeam crew in The Brogue. The Old Brogue, meaning Old Boot was one of the top pubs in Ireland, only matched by Durty Nelly's in Limerick, The Spaniard in Kinsale and Kitty Reilly's Kitchen in County Waterford. Great old-world charm and atmosphere, and always good music.

The Brogue was to become one of our regular haunts. Donnie Houlihan was the manager there and I'd known him for some time. Serica had babysat his children for him and his wife, Theresa, on quite a few occasions, and this always assured us a warm welcome.

Donnie was also well acquainted with Stef who had drunk at The Brogue a lot longer than me. This worried me a little as I wondered if Donnie might quiz Stef on my background. After all, small towns thrive on gossip. But no need for me to worry really because Stef was a seasoned vet on those matters for he had been through that mill on many occasions. Nearly all the commercial travellers in Ireland were having affairs at that time and Stef was better than any Cassius Clay at dodging and weaving.

'Serica, Michael, what are you lads having?'

'A Double Diamond and a Phoenix.' He told me to to put my money back in my pocket. 'Thanks, Donnie. Let's join the girls over there by the fire.'

Marta's first comment was, 'Did she take you to bed?' I smiled a teasing smile, saying nothing. Then a barrage of questions from Marta and the girls. 'What part of Cork are you from? Are you lads going to get engaged? What does your dad do? Are you going to move to Tralee when you get married?' My head was in a whirl. I was saved by the bell.

'Time, ladies and gentlemen. Come on now drink up. The Gardai (Irish policemen) are outside.' We obliged by swigging down our drinks. Everyone said to everyone, 'See you lads later.'

Then I was doing what was fast becoming my favourite pastime: smooching in the red Ford Escort and telling Serica how much I was in love over and over again. When the occasion arose and there was no night porter on at Horans, we would sneak in and practise marriage pleasures and sneak out again. Except for one night when we mistimed our exit and had to climb out the back window and over the wall to avoid being caught. All to keep Serica's reputation intact.

'Michael, are you really serious about this relationship? I know you're always saying you love me, but are you really serious?'

My conscience was again beginning to attack me. I hated this lying thing. 'Of course I am, I swear.' I thought, *I'll tell her the truth next week*. In the next breath I said, 'Serica, I won't be able to see you next week.'

'Why?' came the astonished reply. 'What's wrong?'

'Nothing. It's just that I've got to go to Galway for a week to do some work. I'll ring you during the week to let you know when I'm back.'

'If you're going to be gone for a week I want you to make love to me now and I want you to remember every second of it in the next week while you're away. And, I'll tie a yellow ribbon round the old oak tree for your return.'

I gladly obliged her request. Passionately, in fact. I can certainly vouch for the strength of the springs that Ford put in their Escorts, and the springs would be put to the test on many occasions in the next few months.

I always waited until she closed the door when I dropped her off at home to make sure she was safe inside before I left, but this time I was suffering an attack of the guilts, as she turned back and smiled.

Almost every commercial traveller in Ireland was having an affair in one town or another, and many of them were having multiple affairs—I could certainly vouch for that. I cracked up every Saturday morning when I saw some of them shopping in Patrick Street, Cork, with their wives on their arms and carrying their children.

Several of the lads were having affairs for many years with their intercounty lovers. I suppose I was having the guilts because in the truest sense, I was now no different from the rest of them. Except I didn't want to be like them any more. I wanted in my heart and soul to own up to my deception, but the hypocrisy of Ireland in that day wouldn't allow me to be honest, because if I was I would lose Serica. Everyone in Ireland must've known most travelling reps were having out-of-marriage sex and preferred to turn a blind eye, but the minute any affair became public knowledge then the whole community went into shock. Why?

It was already unofficially accepted in general society and it was no different in the clergy. What else did the priest's housekeepers do other than make his breakfast? Nod-nod, wink-wink. Granted not all, but a hell of a lot of them. No wonder some of them smiled when we called them 'Father'. It was a time of secrets in Ireland and I was just another one with one more, except mine was blowing me apart at the seams. I was head over heels in love in a way I never thought possible.

I felt like a punt on an angry ocean, tossed and battered by the enormous waves of emotion and, as I had never been in a situation like this, I just didn't know how to handle it other than to fall into line with everyone else's attitude. I thought it would sort itself out in time. I was in denial: incapable of understanding the consequences of my behaviour. All I saw was my colleagues and the clergy getting away with having affairs for years, so why not me as well? Why shouldn't I? Except for one thing—the enormous power of love, yes LOVE. Just like an atomic bomb, it was about to destroy me. I had misjudged the power of it and the fundamental difference between the real thing and the loveless affair. And now I was feeling awful about the hypocrisy and the double standards.

After World War II when unemployment in Ireland was sky-high, Irishmen went to England in their thousands looking for work in order to feed their families back home. Lots of them were living double lives, either having affairs or living in de facto relationships, and some didn't return to their wives and families in Ireland ever again. Don't think for a moment it was all one-way traffic. No. What did a huge number of wives do to comfort themselves in the cold lonesome Irish nights?

Do you remember the old saying 'There's a man in the attic'? Well, guess what? There was! Due to the lack of money and need for discretion, the wife couldn't go to a hotel and book a room to share with her lover, so they would go up into the loft and do the dishonour there, hence the noise and the saying to young children at the time, 'If you don't go to sleep the bogey man in the attic will come and get you' . . . And how did they cover up their pregnancies? Of course, the clothing was loose in those days and some wore shawls so it was very hard to pick a pregnant woman.

Now you of innocent minds are thinking, what happens when the child is born, how do you hide it? Well, it was a very well-devised plan. The mother would give the newborn to her girlfriend, whose husband was also in England, and, as the child bore no resemblance to the girlfriend. When the girlfriend's husband came home from England she just told him she adopted the little darling because she was lonesome and the child's teenage mother died, or some other collaborated story. This worked vice versa and God only knows how many children in Ireland were born to lovers in that period of time.

Oh yes, some of the mothers of Ireland are going to have some explaining to do when they get to the pearly gates of heaven (if they have any hope of getting in). It was a conspiracy among sisters and certainly a time of secrets.

❀   ❀   ❀

Even though I regularly cried myself to sleep, hoping it would do something—I'm not sure what, maybe just to make everything better—it never helped.

CHAPTER FOUR

A DOUBLE LIFE

GALWAY IS A BEAUTIFUL place but I wasn't looking forward to going there, for no other reason than I would be on my own again. Galway is just one of the nicest places you could wish to be in: lovely people, fabulous pubs and great eateries, and the countryside has to be seen to be believed. And there I was complaining! I must have had it bad.

The weekend gave me the opportunity to have some catch up time with Liz and Niall, visit Mum and Dad and take in a soccer match—my Cork Hibernians playing Shamrock Rovers. This time I went to the football with Stef only and it also gave me the chance to brief him on my shenanigans in Tralee.

For the rest of the week I sank into my work trying to be normal in between ringing Serica every second night and drinking pints in The Kings Head. In a way, it was a relief not to see her as I didn't have to lie. I was hoping that my abstinence might make it easier for me to get into heaven after all. God was a forgiving God. Anyway, it made me feel good for now and, who knows, I might end up saving someone from a burning wreck or a house-fire one day, and God the all-forgiving would forget about my wayward ways. But then again, wasn't it the Irish who came up with the saying, 'Pigs might fly'? Well, there was no harm in hoping anyway.

Galway came and went without me appreciating it. One of the gems on this earth, but to be honest, I really wasn't able to see or appreciate anything other than Serica. When I returned the pattern of lies and excuses continued and our relationship kept on getting stronger and the passion more intense.

September came with the Rose of Tralee Festival, a week of music and drinking. By now, I was spending almost all of my time in Tralee, neglecting both my children and my work. And due to a shortage of hotel beds Serica senior said I could move in for the week, which I duly obliged. Serica's sister, Nola, and her husband, David, and the granddaughter, Serica, were coming over from England for the festival. We all co-habited fabulously well until Wednesday night when Nola challenged Serica about the suspicious stains on the quilt in their bed, which Serica and I denied emphatically. (It had happened the night before when Serica and I were babysitting young Serica.)

I got the full drill from Nola regarding my future intentions. Of course I was planning to marry Serica, how dare she assume otherwise was my brazen reply. And, as expected, I got a very cold reception for the rest of Nola's stay.

Most of the time, Serica and I socialised with Stef who was also in town for the week. It was much safer for me to be with another couple should I be seen by anyone from Cork, a clever device Stef had cause to use every now and again. The week was a real fun one and everything went well in spite of the stain-on-the-quilt saga. No more of that was mentioned.

Reflecting on my previous trips to Galway I decided to organise a weekend there with Serica. Maybe I would appreciate it more having her with me. The planned date of two weeks hence arrived in no time. I picked her up Friday afternoon and we drove at a leisurely pace to

Limerick, and booked into the Parkway Motel there.

I had to go to the reception desk on my own and booked two rooms. Singles of course, because Serica was embarrassed to be seen in a motel without a wedding ring. We moved our cases into separate rooms until it got dark, then we moved some of her clothes over to my room. She left her case in her own room so she could be seen taking it from there the next morning. So we were spending our first official night together.

We had dinner at the motel and then went into the main ballroom where there was a cabaret and dance. The Parkway had the reputation of being one of the best cabaret and dance venues in Ireland and I can vouch for that for I have been there many times. As a matter of fact, one night the year before I had one of my most embarrassing experiences there.

I was standing at the bar waiting for Stef or Tom or John or any of my commercial traveller friends to arrive. Someone usually turned up—it was a good meeting place on a Monday night. So there I was minding my own business drinking my pint of Double Diamond, when this girl comes up to the bar and asks for a bottle of Bacardi in a slurring voice. I burst out laughing with the contents of my drink in my mouth running down my nose. She turned to me with a bleary look (she had obviously consumed quite a few) and said, 'If you were a gentleman you would buy me a drink. It's my birthday today.'

'Sure,' I said. 'When you finish the bottle why don't you come back and I'll buy you a drink?' So off she went and I resumed my waiting for the lads, drinking and watching the cabaret show. Then to my amazement one hour later, the party girl returned.

'Hey, hunk, are you goin' to buy me that drink now?'

'Sure,' said I. 'Double Bacardi?'

'Yep. Would you like to come over and join my friends and me?'

'No, I'm fine, thank you. You enjoy your drink.'

'But you're on your own and I would like you to join me. You're cute.'

'I'm flattered,' I replied.

'Please come and join us,' she said real sweetly, sobering up momentarily.

'Just for a few minutes,' I said.

As soon as she introduced me to her friends—all eight of them—they commented, 'We know what you're after.' I said, 'I'm leaving,' but she held me tightly and insisted I sit and she sat on my lap. She proceeded to kiss me and her friends continued to taunt me that I was only after one thing. I had no such intention at the time.

When it came to buying drinks, the girl's friends refused to buy me anything and still they continued to taunt me and she continued to kiss me. So after what seemed like hours, even though it was just 30 minutes, I finally broke free and insisted I was leaving. The birthday girl started to cry and argue with her friends. Then she said, 'Will you please take me home?' One of her male friends said, 'I told you, all he wants is to take you home and screw you.' She threw her drink in his face and said to me, 'Let's go.'

We were no sooner out the door when she started kissing me passionately against one of the doorways. It got really hot and in no time at all her knickers and my pants were down around our ankles and my arse was exposed. Just as the moment of ejaculation was arriving came the loud comments from behind me, 'What did I tell you? He was only after one thing.' I was literally caught with my pants down.

I ran through the car park looking for my car, pulling up my pants and ransacking my pockets for the keys. *What will my mother say if she finds out?* I had visions of my body being found in the car park with my trousers still knotted around my ankles. However, all's well that ends well. I made it to the safety of my car and sped off. And I never saw her or her friends again. I never even knew her name.

Going from the ridiculous to the sublime: on another occasion I arrived at this wonderful venue, again on a Monday night, to be greeted by Stef and a group of fellow commercial travellers accompanied by a face I had never seen before. My colleagues introduced him to me as an apprentice up-and-coming jockey. After dinner and a few drinks we all wandered into the Monday night cabaret.

I mentioned to the lads that I had acquired some condoms and asked if they needed any. I got a chorus of 'Yes!' The young apprentice was sheepish in putting his hand out to receive his allocation of illicit contraception for condoms were contraband in Ireland. Anyone found bringing them into the country or distributing them was looked upon as being equivalent to a drug dealer such was the enormous control that the Church had over state matters. (The Church was wielding its power over the state to enforce its rules, yet the Vatican had huge amounts of monies invested in manufacturing contraceptives. Hypocrisy of the highest order.) However, on this particular Monday night at the Parkway Motel the Vatican and its hypocrisy was far from our minds and a good time was had by all. I was assured by my colleagues that the population of Ireland remained unchanged mainly due to the illicit contraband.

On arrival at the dining room to join my colleagues for breakfast, I was greeted with wild laughter. I went red in the face, thinking my fly was open or something worse. What could it be? Finally, I was informed that the young apprentice jockey had put his condom on just after receiving it and was still wearing it, the poor innocent slob. Then the laughter escalated as Stef shouted out that the jockey was the only one who didn't get a ride last night. The poor lad was so embarrassed, but he did go on to be one of Ireland's top jockeys, and got many rides and winners of a different kind throughout his career.

The circumstances were so very different when I went there with Serica. No quickie knee-tremblers or wild chases in the car park. With Serica, I felt like the luckiest fellow in the world. There was nowhere else I'd rather have been or anyone else I'd rather have been with than Serica, not for all the tea in China or all the money in Fort Knox. This was it.

We met some local girls and told them we were on a trial honeymoon. We shared their table and local gossip. We encouraged them to come and dance with us. All Serica's favourites were being played: Gary Glitter's 'Hello, Hello, I'm Back', 'I'm the Leader of the Gang', the Carpenters' 'Yesterday Once More' and lots of Tom Jones favourites. But the night would not have been complete without 'Tie a Yellow Ribbon Round the Old Oak Tree', by special request.

We couldn't control the anticipation any more and we bid our new friends goodbye and headed for the so-called honeymoon suite—a single bed, in a tiny room. But that didn't matter to us. We couldn't wait to share our feelings in the most intimate fashion. No hiding behind country fences in the car or sneaking past the night porter, just sharing love in its most pure form.

I woke to Serica frantically searching the bed. 'Jesus, Michael, I lost one of my contact lenses, I forgot to take them out last night.' We stripped the bed, searched everywhere without any luck. As the panic died down and Serica headed for the bathroom, in the faint light I noticed a flicker on the left cheek of her bum. Sure enough there was the missing culprit firmly stuck to it. We both broke into fits of laughter. How it got there left us mystified.

We packed our bags, had breakfast and headed north to Galway.

The Ennis Road is beautiful to drive on, the best in Ireland. I should know, I drove them all. We passed Bunratty Castle and Durty Nelly's along the Serine Road that goes through the beautiful town of Ennis in County Clare. I knew Ennis very well as I had worked there many times in my days with Irish Roofing.

I remember Mathew Gough and I once worked on the roof of the Old Ground Hotel for two weeks. Mat was a real character. Every night when we would be heading off for a few drinks or to a dance, Mat would stand in front of the mirror patting his face with Old Spice and say to himself, 'Well, Mat, whose heart are you going to break tonight? Ah ha! Your own again. Gee, man, you're a sucker for punishment.'

On the day we finished the job on the hotel, some American tourists asked if they could film us on the roof. Mat said, 'Sure,' and whispered to me, 'They think we're leprechauns, stupid bastards.' Then one asked Mat if he could film the funeral that was taking place across the road in the church. 'Of course you can,' said Mat, 'No problem. Boy, they'd love that.' Then he muttered to me, 'Best get the fuck out of here 'cause when he finds out it's an IRA funeral we shouldn't be around.'

As we drove out the gate, the hotel manager complemented us on a fine job well done and asked, 'Will the roof always look this good?' to which Mat proudly replied, grinning from ear to ear, 'Sure, providing you paint it every day.' We drove away swiftly. Looking in my rear-view mirror, I saw the crowd outside the church were tearing at the Yank's clothing and kindly showing him how to drop-kick a camera . . .

I would be taking a wide berth around the Old Ground today. We turned off to Milltown Malbay, drove up the coast through Lahinch and stopped to admire the Cliffs Of Moher. Then through Lisdoonvarna, and a stop at Fanore Bridge to gaze at the Aran Islands. Ireland certainly has been given an abundance of beauty, and history has shown it's cost many a heartache and its fair share of good men to keep it, no thanks to our neighbours.

On to Ballyvaughan, Oranmore and in no time we were in Galway. Everywhere was booked, so we headed for Salthill and found a place in the Warwick Hotel. Same story: I did the booking as Serica wouldn't approach the reception desk without a wedding ring. She was so embarrassed. I told her to keep her left hand in her pocket and she smiled.

'Room seven, Mr and Mrs Bowen.'

The porter offered to carry our bags and we struggled over them. I was quicker and stronger and he surrendered sheepishly. Anyway, I neither wanted nor could afford to tip him. I remembered my mother saying to me years ago, 'You should never ask or pay anybody to do something that you can do yourself.' As I watched Serica unpack I felt like I was in God's own parlour, warm and snuggly safe.

But life is not all about sweetness and roses and I was just about to find out. Serica turned to me white as milk and clutching her stomach.

She groaned, 'You'd better get me to a doctor.'

Oh, shit, Christ, fuck. 'What's wrong, are you alright?' *What am I saying? Of course she's not alright otherwise she wouldn't look like a ghost. Panic, panic. What happens if she dies on me. Oh God, I hate you. I suppose this is your way of punishing me as if I haven't enough torment in my life as it is. God you can be cruel sometimes.*

'Will you be able to walk to the car?' She held my arm and dragged herself there. I ran back into the reception area to get the address of the nearest doctor.

I sat in the waiting room like an expectant father, cursing and praying for God to make her OK. I promised Him anything, even if He wanted me to become a priest. Just save her and, of course, I will tell her the whole truth about myself as long as He made her better. Nothing else mattered to me. My only thoughts were, *Lord don't punish her, only me, only me, please.*

By now I was distraught with guilt and in a flood of tears. The nurse asked me if I was alright and I was unable to answer. Then the doctor and Serica appeared after what seemed like a very long time and the doctor said, 'She's got food poisoning.'

'Does that mean she's going to die, Doctor?'

'No,' he replied.

We spent the rest of the weekend confined to the hotel room and I nursed and catered for her every need. I cherished each moment pampering her. There was so much of Galway I wanted to show her and impress her with, but that had to wait for another time. (I kept wondering if there would be another time.) We watched the sun go down on Galway Bay through our hotel room window and I began to worry that my luck was running out on me. I was feeling the puppet master was going to have me dancing to a different tune in the not-too-distant future.

I was broken hearted as we left Galway. I had so wanted Serica to enjoy the trip and I had been hoping I would be able to tell her of my secret, but the timing was again all wrong. Surely it wasn't expected of me to tell her now, now that she wasn't well. Don't tell me that God expected me to stick to a promise I made when I was totally out of my mind with worry and only concerned about someone else and not myself. I guess I was using every excuse again for not telling the truth.

We headed down through County Clare to Kilrush, crossed the ferry to Tarbert through Listowel, but not before stopping at John B. Keane's place for a few drinks. John B. was one of Ireland's most prominent writers and one hell of a character. He owned and ran one of the best pubs in Ireland.

We reached Tralee at dark. I was again confronted with the same old demons: was this going to be my last weekend experiencing the pinnacle of love? Who knows, I could only keep my fingers crossed and pray like hell that my secret remained a secret until I told her, and hopefully no one would tell her before me.

My attention was brought back to reality as Serica sang Peter and Lee's 'Welcome Home', ever so sweetly. She had my instant attention. Off went the radio. (Sorry Gary Glitter, even if you are the leader of the gang.)

I stopped the car in the middle of Edward Street in Tralee, reached over and drew her to me and kissed the most beautiful girl in the world passionately for what seemed like forever and a day until all the cars behind me started tooting angrily. Well, to hell with them, if they were in my position they would be mad not to be doing what I was doing.

Then an angry face pressed up against the windscreen and said, 'Are you going to fuckin' move or am I going to do it for you?' I'll bet you Batman and Robin never got to the speed I got to leaving Edward Street in my Ford Escort!

We played out the usual pub crawl routine that night, then back to Horans to make love till early morning. Then came the heart wrenching goodbyes and I was alone again wondering if it was all a dream, and would I ever see her again?

Well, it sure as hell was nearly the last I was to see of her, for on my way home to Cork the next morning caught up in reminiscing, I failed to observe the train going through the Farranfore crossing and it was only a miracle that I wasn't made a permanent feature of the roadway. I had visions of the CIE railway staff scraping me off the road with an egg turner.

I sat in shock at the wheel, trembling in a trance. Finally I came to my senses and moved to the side of the road, thanked God for my life, and wondered if it was a sign of some sort. I got out of the car and sat on the side of the road crying uncontrollably. I didn't know if it was because of the near-accident or the awful double life I was living which sure as hell was taking its toll on me. My strong work ethic was slipping and my work rate was down. My time with the children was suffering, my relationship with Mum and Dad wasn't good because I was constantly having to defend myself for spending more and more time away from home. Stef was continuously worried about my wayward ways. He was forever telling me it was only a matter of time before the shit hit the fan or I'd burn myself out. 'Go ahead,' he said, 'blow your own fucking brains out, boy, because what you're doing is the same thing anyway, only slower.'

The noise from the goods train passing brought my mind back to the present, I wiped my eyes and dried my tears, jumped back in the car and headed for Cork.

I met Stef for coffee to discuss the events of the weekend. Cork was typical Cork that morning—rain, rain and more rain—but that's Cork: gloomy but beautiful in its own way. And no matter where you park in Cork you don't have far to go to in order to find a good pub.

The Long Valley pub was the ideal haven for me to confide my secrets to Stef. It felt warm and cosy.

Stef went to great lengths to explain to me the 'Code of the Road'.

'You can have as many affairs as you like, but remember, you can't afford to fall in love 'cos it will only get you into trouble. Love always does. And it's a no-no to speak of any infidelity that happens on the road. Simple. You understand?' he asked, poking his fingers into my armpit. 'Them are the rules.'

'Stef, I'm physically and mentally drained. I know what I should do and I know what I can't do.'

'Why don't you spend a bit of time at home with the children and work locally and then after a month or so, if you find you can't settle down you could spend a few weeks on the road with me. I'm sure that would take your mind off her. At least you owe it to the children to give it a try.'

As difficult as it seemed, I knew he was right. I made the necessary excuses to Serica to cover my absence for a month or so.

I loved everything about the children: their sweet smell, their cries, feeding them, taking Niall to school and picking him up afterwards. I loved the gobbley-goo talk and all of that made it harder for me to understand why I couldn't have a normal life. Of course, the problem was not the children, it was the mismatch of Mary and myself, the environment of home and the wet beds.

I loved and hated being home. I loved every second of the children and hated everything else. I had managed, due to some sort of miracle, to keep my thoughts of Serica and communications with her to a minimum. But a month was really all I could manage before Mary and I nearly started World War III. As promised to Stef, I spent the next two weeks on the road with him, working hard during the day and living hard at night without stress or worry, but still I just couldn't wait for the two weeks to end so I could return to Tralee. It was still my drug and she my all-consuming fix.

I knew my time with Serica was finally coming to a conclusion. I could almost smell it. It was so close.

CHAPTER FIVE

WHAT GOES UP MUST COME DOWN

IT HAD BEEN rumoured among Serica's friends that we may be getting engaged for Christmas. I'm sure she encouraged the rumours to pin me down, and I don't blame her. God knows, I didn't dispel the comments either, I just side-stepped the questions.

My heart moved up a beat as I headed for Kerry, and as Charlie Rich so beautifully put it, towards 'The Most Beautiful Girl in the World'. The adrenaline rush was so intense, I felt I was floating to Tralee instead of driving. My excitement moved up another notch as Tony Orlando blasted out 'Tie a Yellow Ribbon Round the Old Oak Tree' when I drove through Killarney. And, as if to taunt me, or test me or just to prove a point that coincidences do happen, Peters and Lee just about knocked my socks off with 'Welcome Home'. The tears flowed, I felt this was going to be my best or worst trip to Tralee.

As soon as I saw that beautiful face and the gorgeous red hair, that fabulous smile and those cute glasses I knew I just loved her more than anything and she didn't have to say a word because she just glowed. It was the first time I had seen another person's aura. We just held each other and squeezed and I never wanted to let go. Something in the back of my mind told me to savour every moment as there might not be too many left. I can still feel it today all these years later.

The week consisted of hard work during the day (I was firing again on all cylinders), lots of pub crawling at night, and the essence of love-making at every opportunity. We did it on Banna Beach, the back seat of the red Escort, and Horans Hotel—I don't think we missed too many places. As an added spice, Serica's birthday was on Thursday. That day was special. I gave her some money and she bought a leather jacket. She had impeccable taste and it looked fabulous on her. Again, all that week, I avoided the questions on engagement.

To appreciate the ups in life you have to experience the downs. My downs were in the form of the approaching weekend when I had to be back at the office on Saturday morning.

I dropped Serica home at 4.00 am precisely on Saturday morning after one of the most fabulous weeks of my life. We promised nothing would ever stop us from being together, which now set the scene for me to break the news to her on my next trip. I was feeling at long last I could get some sort of relief from my guilt; confident that when I returned to Tralee the next Wednesday, by Thursday this ten-tonne weight of guilt would be gone and I—we—could seriously start to plan a new life together.

No doubt we would have to move to England to escape the prejudice in Ireland. But then again that could be dangerous as I could be extra-dited back to Ireland for deserting a marriage which is a prison offence in Ireland. And divorce is not an option, mainly because of the Catholic Church stronghold. So the only viable option would be to use England as a stepping-stone to move on to a safe haven—that is, a country that did not have an extradition treaty with Ireland. We would have to stay away from Ireland for twelve years, according to the statute of limitations. At least this was the information on the streets. I certainly wasn't going to bring attention to my own cause by formal-ly enquiring.

I didn't care if we lived on the moon as long as we were together. Of course, there was going to be problems with Mary and the children, but I was prepared for that, or so I thought. My mother would be outraged: 'You made a mistake marrying Mary, now you have to live with it. I married your father and that was a mistake and I have lived with mine.' My father would understand, he would be upset but he would know it was best. He understood how passionate I could be about some things and he would know there would be no changing my mind once it was made up.

I crawled into bed at about four-thirty, hoping for some sleep before heading for Cork. It was a fruitless effort, too many thoughts going through my head. At least I got three hours rest if not sleep.

I never enjoyed the trips back to Cork because it reminded me of going back and not forward. Back to the city of my poverty-stricken youth, my dyslexia, my broken marriage. Going back scared me. All my imperfections were in Cork, all of my failures. The rat-infested, three-storey flats that I grew up in were in Cork. The North Infirmary Hospital was there and, worst of all, The New School still stood in Cathedral Road where I constantly got put to the back of the class because I couldn't spell.

I never forgave God for giving me dyslexia because it made me feel such a fool and everyone saw it simply as an excuse not to learn. See, it's different if you have a cold or a scab, people can relate to that, but not if you have dyslexia. I promised one day I would be coming to Cork for better times, not going back to Cork for the bad times.

It rained all the way which made the journey even more glum. For some strange reason I began to think that because of all the traumas in my life, God owed me a brilliant future, and why not? If he was a fair God he would surely want to balance the books. For all the hungry days my sister and I had; for all the Sundays when there was only soup to eat; for all the times my feet got cold and wet from the hand-me-down shoes, all holed and worn; for all the looks I never got from girls because we were poor and different; for all the times I was ridiculed because my father was a drunk and sang Mario Lanza songs as loud as he could all the way home from the pub; for all the times I couldn't bring a girl home because I was ashamed of the place and afraid that my father would fall in the front door roaring drunk.

St. Finbars Hospital was also in Cork and it scared me every time I passed it, for I didn't have pleasant memories of my twelve months there as a child-patient. When it was decided by the brains-that-be in the medical world that I would have to go into hospital again because of my recurring bronchitis and pneumonia, the North Infirmary was full so I had to spend my time in St Finbars, often referred to as 'The Union' because of the amount of women working in its laundry. And it also had become infamous because of the whole religious laundry affair in Ireland—now commonly know as the Magdalene Sisters scandal.

St. Finbars was a forbidding, isolated place for a young child to spend time. If it sounds like an institution, it was. The food was terrible, I know because I wasn't used to much in the way of food, and this was still awful stuff! The nurses were kept on their feet by their superiors: staff nurses who behaved like little Hitlers as they administered their orders. And if a caring nurse was generous to me with time or affection, she would get a devil of a look from the little Hitler and then have to rush off to attend other matters.

I didn't have the luxury of my Aunt Mary to visit me daily as she previously did in the North Infirmary. As a matter of fact, I rarely had a visitor as Liza was also in hospital and Mick was busy drinking and my poor soul mate Breda was in and out of hospital herself with rheumatic fever, though she did manage to visit me in between her own stints in hospital. Liza would occasionally write a letter to me but as I couldn't read, and rarely would any of the staff read her letters for me. I was very much alone.

I had only ever been isolated as a child on one other occasion—equally bad, if not worse—when I spent eight weeks as one of only two patients in the Fever Hospital, when the North Infirmary was full again.

Not a lot of consideration was given to educating children who spent long periods of time in hospital and no time was given to keep children occupied during the long, boring Irish winters. And so this was life for me in St. Finbars until a Mr. Maurice Hickey picked up my medical records from the end of my bed by mistake one day.

'Who's looking after this young man, nurse?' he shouted.

'I think it's Doctor—' but before she had time to mention the doctor's name he said, 'I'll see this young man on my Monday rounds.' And so I acquired one of the best surgeons in Ireland.

Monday morning and true to his word. 'Good morning, young man,' he said to me firmly. 'My name's Mr Hickey, Maurice Hickey. You have been a very sick young man for a very long time and I'm going to make you better, OK?'

All I could think of was, *Get me out of here, the sooner the better and I don't care what they have to do.* 'OK by me, Doc.'

Doctor Hickey turned to the nurse and said, 'Nurse, contact his parents, we will operate on him this Thursday week.' And again true to his word, Doctor Maurice Hickey used his medical skills on my delicate and feeble seven-year-old body, removing the major part of my left lung.

One way to spoil a seven-year-old patient is to put him in a girls ward to recover from his major operation and give him his own nurse to sit by his bed and read him stories. This way you surely have a happy patient in spite of all the pain and tubes going in and out of his body. I loved the attention, and the recovery was going to plan until the third day after the operation just after the medical staff removed the intravenous tubes from my hands and back.

I leaned over to put a little toy army tank that I was playing with into my locker and all hell broke loose. Nurses, staff doctors and nuns started running everywhere, everyone seemed to go into panic mode. I kept asking what was wrong but no one was answering. I couldn't understand all the fuss.

The events that followed played on my mind for twenty years before

I could speak of what happened, adding another secret to my life. It was only in 1976 when I read a copy of *On Death and Dying* by Elizabeth Kubler-Ross, that I was able to reveal my experience of that day in St. Finbars Hospital. You see, I was petrified that people might think, 'That kid's bonkers,' and I'm sure that was what any one would have said until Elizabeth Kubler-Ross opened the Pandora's box on out-of-body experiences. Because that's what happened to me . . .

As I bent over my locker, my vision of what was happening changed. I moved from the pillow-end of my bed to about four feet off the ground at the foot of my bed. I was suspended in mid-air in the sitting position observing the nurses and doctors working on my body trying to revive me. The nun in charge had her right hand opened across the front of my head bending me forward as she slapped me on the back, and shouting, 'Don't sleep, you must fight, son, you can't die.' She was weeping with rage and desperation. Meanwhile, a nurse was inserting an intravenous needle into my right arm while a doctor was cutting out a slice from my left wrist to insert another much longer needle into my left arm. He started pumping blood from an attached bottle into me. Another hole was cut into my back so the old or bad blood would flow out into a long bottle under my bed.

I was fascinated watching all this excitement and action; just like watching a movie. But there were no trips up a tunnel to meet God or bright lights or signs or anything like that; it wasn't my time yet.

'Come on now, young man we can't have any of that here,' I heard Mr Hickey's voice say as he turned me on my side. He looked into my eyes and said, 'Now listen here, young man, I promised to make your life better and you're not going to let me down are you?' He then asked the nun to leave us for a minute. 'All of those wonderful people worked very hard to keep you alive especially the Sister over there because they know you're special. Not everyone gets to survive and you have this special privilege so you get yourself back here now so those people can feel proud that they did a great job for you.'

From that moment on the spirit and the body became one again and

Mr Hickey smiled and squeezed my hand. Turning to the nun he said, 'Sister, your patient is back now, you did a wonderful job. Thank you.' She bowed gracefully to Mr Hickey, 'Yes, sir.' He then turned, winked at me, and walked off and St. Finbars returned to normal.

I remember almost everything in detail as if it were only yesterday. Out-of-body experiences were not a subject to be discussed in my time as a child in Ireland, so a secret it remained for many years.

Cork was also the scene of my shame when I left school. They told me I would amount to nothing as I only spent five-and-a-half years there and couldn't read or write. I cursed my dyslexia even though I had no idea what it was other than a fool's illness that no one understood. And to make my departure worse, they wouldn't let me join the school band because I was tone deaf. What an attitude to have!

I was broken hearted because I just loved music, it is the caviar of the poor and I was deprived of even that. Of course, what they didn't understand was that staying in or leaving school wasn't a choice I could make. Leaving school was a necessity of the highest order. It was about survival. My father was in the pubs constantly and my mother was in and out of sanatoriums with tuberculosis, and my sister had rheumatic fever of the heart, which put her in hospital regularly. Only when she was at home could she fend for me. Basically, it was she and I against the elements living on our survival skills.

My Aunt Mary was my guardian angel, she was so, so special in my younger years. If it wasn't for her, I can't imagine what might have been. She was the one who showed me there was light at the end of the tunnel, she was the one who gave me the will to fight and reminded me over and over again that I would go on to be very successful. She was the one who gave me my most precious quote: 'Mike, you may be born into shit but you don't have to live in it. You have the choice. Now go out there and make a name for yourself.'

Aunt Mary worked in the laundry at the North Infirmary Hospital and it was she who brought me lollies and a smile every day while I was in hospital there. She had a very distinct cough, and I could hear her as she delivered fresh sheets and pillowcases to the other wards. That gave me comfort knowing she was near, I knew a kiss and a hug was on its way.

When God put man on this earth, he made a special category for people like Aunt Mary; the unselfish people who give and give and don't want anything in return. Right now, I was being selfish to say the least. The arrogance I possessed—how dare I demand anything of God? I decided that only when I begin to understand other people's dilemmas and to learn to give and think more of others, maybe then life would turn around for me. After all, there are thousands, if not millions, of people who were worse off than me.

With Aunt Mary's words in my ears I made up my mind: I would tell Serica on Wednesday.

There was no letting up of the rain as I approached Cork, so it seemed like a good idea to catch up with Stef, bleed my heart out over a few pints, then go home after the rest of the family had gone to bed.

I woke up the next morning still remembering Stef's astonished look, 'Are you fucking mad? You're going to tell her?' 'Yeah,' I said with a smile, thinking of the relief that I would have from the guilt. Even making the decision lifted a huge weight from my shoulders. I hadn't felt that calm for a long, long time.

So it was the usual routine when in Cork for the weekend: Clancy's in Oliver Plunket Street for a few pints on Saturday and a catch up with all the boys for the gossip and news and a slag. Then, the Blue Heaven Bar in Kinsale on Saturday night, a game of 'Pitch and Put' on Sunday morning before the pubs opened, then to watch Cork Celtic (Cork Hibbs were playing away). The only reason we even went to see Celtic was because Paddy Short played with them. He was a brilliant player, way ahead of his time and, in our younger days, Paddy and I were in the same class in school. We were also in the Boy Scouts together and it was great to see one of my old schoolmates do so well, I always felt proud of him. But Hibbs were still my team, and that was where my loyalty lay.

When Dave Becuzzi became player manager of Cork Hibbs he

changed the entire face of soccer in Ireland. He made Hibbs into a really professional team and set a new benchmark in the sport. I understand one of his comments when he took over was, 'We will play in white stripes, we will look, play and conduct ourselves in a professional manner just like the best team on earth, Real Madrid.' So he proceeded about his task by recruiting some of the most exciting players ever to be seen in the League of Ireland. There was David Wiggington, Carl Davenport, John Lawson, Jerry Marsden, just to name a few. And, of course, Dave was a class player himself having played in the top grade in England with Arsenal in the first division.

Everything about Dave was professional and classy and it wasn't on soccer alone that he made such an impact. His influence also carried over to the greater majority of the population of Cork City; igniting a whole new spark of enthusiasm among the locals. Cork was and still is a huge Gaelic Athletic Association (GAA) loyal county, having enormous success in hurling and giving rise to icons such as Christy Ring and Jack Lynch. Yet, in spite of this, and an unfair ban put in place by the GAA (that anyone, male or female, who played the native games but attended a foreign game, like soccer or rugby, would be banned from playing for them), it was still very unusual not to see large numbers of members of that Association at the Hibbs games, such was their pulling power. So it was middle finger up to the GAA and when it became known that the great Kerry footballer, Mick O'Connell, had attended a Hibbs game, rather than ban the great icon, the rules were finally eased.

Dave presided over Hibbs's most successful years and ordered his players to be professional both on and off the field. His understanding of the game was way ahead of his time. I wonder if he ever fully understood the impact he had on the sporting public of Cork and I for one hope Cork honours this man one day with the highest accolade for his profession. History should be very generous to Dave Becuzzi.

Monday morning was typical Cork autumn: fog and cold mist, a vest inside your shirt and maybe an overcoat. At the same time something else was happening that wasn't at all typical, which would change my life forever . . .

I went about my normal duties. Taking Niall to school, then the cup of tea or coffee with Stef and the boys to check what they were up to and where they were going to be that week. Stef wished me luck before I left and asked me to promise to let him know how I got on as soon as I told Serica. 'Of course I will,' I assured him, 'first thing Thursday morning.'

'No, no,' he replied. 'Wednesday after you talk to her, OK?'

'Yes, OK OK,' I assured him.

I arrived at the office to a distressed receptionist who said a woman rang and left a message to tell me I was a miserable, lying bastard and hoped I would die roaring in hell. No name, no phone number. I might not be the wisest man God put on this earth, but I could still tell it wasn't an admirer.

I tried to convince myself it must be a mistake of identity or wrong number. Just to be on the safe side I thought I would ring Serica at Horans Hotel that night. I knew she would be there with Marta, Marion and the other girls having drinks and a post-mortem of the weekend, and no doubt the girls would be posing the question, 'Serica, when are you lads getting married?'

The phone seemed to ring forever before someone answered. I asked for Serica, the male voice said, 'She doesn't want to talk to you,' and hung up. I rang back immediately, my heart racing at a hundred miles an hour. I was in overdrive. This time it was a female voice, same reply.

'Don't hang up,' I pleaded. 'Please, please don't hang up. I know she knows, I know everyone knows, that's why she won't talk to me.' The tears were pouring down my face and I was pleading to the woman to let me explain and comfort Serica. I could only imagine how hurt she must have been and the pain and shame of everyone in Tralee knowing no doubt long before she did. She must have been in agony knowing the gossipers would be having a field day that Serica was having an affair with a man married with children from Cork. I was crouched down in the foetal position in the telephone booth crying and arguing and begging the voice to let me talk to and comfort my Serica.

I felt helpless and angry with myself for not telling her what happened. Who told her? Didn't they know I was the one to tell her, how dare they? Who gave them the right to squeal? Didn't they know that things have got to be done in a dignified way, not by whispers or back-door methods? Logic had completely gone out the window and only panic and chaos remained.

'SERICA, SERICA, I LOVE YOU,' I screamed down the line, as I lay huddled on the rain-soaked floor of the telephone box. The voice told me Serica was coming to the phone.

'Serica, Serica, I'm sorry,' I cried.

'And so you should be, you fucking bastard. You fucking miserable bastard. I hope you rot in hell,' she screamed.

'Please, please, let me explain,' I pleaded. She hung up. I rang back. A voice said, 'Get fucked.' I was. My thoughts raced by a million a second. I couldn't go home then, not tonight anyway, not in that state. I was a wreck.

I was right about my apprehension in going back to Cork. If I'd stayed in Tralee for the weekend this wouldn't have happened. *Now I have another miserable memory of Cork,* I told myself.

I headed for Joe Rice's place. I knew he would be happy to come and get drunk with me and listen to my whingeing as long as I was paying for the drink. Stef, my soulmate, was in Galway, otherwise he would have had to put up with me.

Joe and I drank ourselves stupid in the Ardmaning pub until they threw us out. God knows what we drank or how I drove back to Joe's place, it was a complete blackout. The massive headache and sick feeling from the alcohol along with the awful guilt, didn't give me a bright start the next morning. Joe's Breda made me a cup of tea and sent me on my way. Funny how we think a good night on the drink will make everything alright tomorrow. It's a fool's paradise because tomorrow comes and you still have to face the music.

I looked into the mirror and the person there looked just like my father but with a more expensive suit. Oh, how I had been deceiving myself and everyone else.

'Jesus, boy, what did you expect?' came Stef's reply when I told him. 'If you wouldn't tell her, it was only a matter of time before some jealous bastard who wanted to jump into her knickers would tell her. Surely you understood that you stupid shagger, didn't you? You should have told her up front, for chrisakes, and then if she agreed to go along with it you wouldn't be in the shit now, would you?'

'For fuck's sake, Stef, what was I supposed to say? "Oh, Serica, I really fancy you, do you mind having dinner with me and maybe jump in the back seat of the Escort for a shag afterwards? Oh, and by the way, I'm married with two kids, but I'm sure that won't bother you because if it does I'll just go away." Stef, I did what I thought was right at the time. I sincerely never meant to hurt her. I fell in love in a huge way like I never thought anyone could, Stef. For as true as God be my judge, I've never loved anyone like that in my life. You know that, don't you?'

My knees were giving out and I found myself slumping to the ground and the tears were flowing like the Cork winter's rain.

'How, Stef, how will she ever know the truth?'

He helped me to my feet and whispered, 'Somehow, I don't think it really matters now because she's angry and everyone around her is telling her you're a lying bastard so I don't think you can talk to her for a long, long time. That is, if she'll ever talk to you again. I'm afraid you're going to have to live with the pain of this for a very long time, boy, if you were that much in love, that's the price you have to pay.'

'What do I do, Stef? I just can't go back to so-called normal living at home, can I? I'll go nuts.'

We were interrupted by some girls moving to sit at the next table. 'How's it going there lads?' One of them smiled one of those smiles. 'Well there's your answer,' he grinned, 'Keep yourself busy with all the other fish in the sea.' Then he asked, 'What about that other chick you were in love with in Limerick. What was her name—Marion?'

'I suppose that was one of the reasons I never told Serica I was married. Remember, I was dating Marion for about a year and I never, never had sex with her, not once.'

I told him how she was just a lovely lady, though I didn't know what to call that relationship, I suppose it was just a very, very respectful one and great fun with no pressure. It grew into love, and then one day I drove from Cork to Limerick to pick her up from work to take her to dinner and then back to work afterwards. Then I decided to stay over. And when I went to pick her up that evening to go to Durty Nelly's (our favourite pub) she was standing by the gate at the end of the pathway to her house. She greeted me with a peck on the cheek. Then she leaned over the gate and whispered for me to look over her right shoulder to the top window of her house. 'Dad's standing there and he's got a gun aimed at you. He said to tell you if you try to move one foot from the gate with me, you're history.'

I muttered softly, 'Jesus, Marion. What did I do?'

'You didn't do anything, darling,' she smiled, 'I did.'

'So why is the gun pointing at me?'

'Because I'm his daughter and he's not going to shoot me, now is he?'

'What in the name of God did you do that was so bad?'

'I told him you were married.'

'Christ, Marion, did you tell him we didn't have sex?'

'Of course I did, do you think I'm silly? But do you think he would believe me? Oh, no, parents don't always believe their children do they? And, of course, he told my mum and she told my sisters.'

'Do you want me to talk to him?'

'I think he would sooner shoot you rather than listen to you at the moment, darling.'

'Surely there's something I can do.'

'He won't let me see you again. No point in arguing and I can't go against his wishes. I will always love you, Mike. Please, go before he gets impatient and pulls the trigger. Ring me now and again to let me know how you are. And don't forget to ask me, "What are you doing Sunday?"' That was her favourite song. Tony Orlando's music sure had an influence on the women in my life.

She was such an amazing lady, so dignified, so elegant, so charming. I was broken hearted, a real wreck after that relationship. She was everything I had wished and hoped for.

I remember well the first time I laid eyes on her in the Parkway Motel at the Monday night cabaret. She was glowing, her smile lit up the whole place; such poise, such innocence and grace. I was at the bar and she was ordering drinks for herself and friends and without even asking, I found myself shouting to the barman, 'That's my call.' Thinking to myself, 'Oh, shit, what if she tells me to get lost? I'll be stuffed before I even get a word in.' I stood in suspense and sure enough the reaction was, 'Would you like to join me and my friends?' Would I what!

She immediately told me, 'You can't take me home as I have to leave with my friends.' But not to be outfoxed I quickly told her that there was no problem as I had a minibus and would be only too happy to see that they all got home safely. 'Of course, you'll be the last one I'll be dropping home.' No objection came my way so we lapped up the fun atmosphere of the night until it was time to go and, as promised, I delivered everyone home safely and Marion last.

Once we kissed, I just melted in her arms. Twelve months of innocent love, of just being together, dancing, movies, walking, it didn't matter, we just loved being together. But sadly, never to go further because of my situation. I felt like a monster with this millstone of a sham marriage around my neck—a stigma that stained every woman that got close to me or who had the misfortune to love me. How I craved for a normal and loving relationship. So I made a mistake in marriage, a mistake that looks like haunting me forever, a dungeon with no exit door.

'Yes Stef, she was a fabulous lady and what happened when I was being noble and truthful? I nearly get me fucking head blown off. Now do you understand why I was so scared to tell Serica? So much for being truthful. If that could happen to me when I wasn't even having sex (a miracle in itself) I wasn't going to risk telling Serica until the time was perfect.'

'But, you stupid bastard, you waited too long and someone else got under your guard and that's why you're here today in the condition you're in, and someone else is shagging her, I bet you. My suggestion is just go and shag every old doll you can get your hands on and you'll get over it because you've got no choice. You can cry yourself stupid and whinge all you like but you have fuck-all hope of trying to make up so do yourself a favour, screw yourself silly and forget about her.'

I knew I couldn't just sit around and brew about Serica for I was positive I'd go mad. So I wasn't left with any option but to take Stef's advice, it was either that or back to the regular arguments with Mary and the wet beds. The choice was obvious.

When I left Stef I felt somewhat happier in a strange way. And off I set, to try and shag every girl in Ireland just to help me get over Serica. I suppose most fellows would be happy with that sort of job and I suppose you could say it was better than sweeping the streets for the Cork County Council, for there I was going about what most fellows would kill to do. But oh no, not me. I must be eleven pence short of a shilling—what was wrong with me? *C'mon son*, I told myself. *Remember, the times you were an ugly duckling, well, now's the time to make up for all that.* From November 1973 to May 1974 I don't think there was a woman I spoke to that I didn't go to bed with.

One night the Grand Hotel had their Christmas dinner and I was invited to accompany one of the barmaids, whose name I'd sooner not mention as I think I caused her enough shame already. Earlier that day I had put some money on a horse and to my amusement he shit in at a huge price. So I was straight on the phone to Stef and headed for Horans in Killarney for a belly-full of Double Diamond. Of course, booze is the ideal recipe to throw timing and logic out the window so Stef and I arrived in Tralee late and drunk as skunks.

I changed my clothes and tried to spruce up my face, which looked like a dartboard after my attempt at shaving. I couldn't figure out why my date didn't wait. After all, I was only an hour and forty-five minutes late. I got a lift from one of the other guests at the hotel to the venue as Stef had other plans.

I virtually fell in the door, with a big drunken smile. 'How are you?' My date ignored me. So I stumbled to my chair and picked up two tickets in front of my plate. As I tried to focus on them, I heard a voice say, '. . . And the winning number is seven.' I couldn't believe it, I was holding the winning ticket and I hadn't yet put my arse on the chair. Geez, I was having a lucky day. And the voice said, 'The prize is two bottles of wine.' Oh, Christ, as if I didn't have enough to drink. I was sure I'd drunk enough to refloat the Titanic. Oh well, what's another few drinks when you're already pissed? So off with the tops and I was like a priest serving out communion in between slugging from the bottle. Not that anyone minded for chrisakes, wasn't it a free drink anyway?

I remember spending most of the night threatening the chef because he was chatting up my date and there was no way I wanted that culchie bastard shagging her. As for her, she totally avoided me all night and, come to think of it, I don't blame her. I wouldn't want to spend my night with a pathetically drunk woman either!

Nevertheless, I was not going to miss out on a shag, so when we got back to the Grand after the function (of which I don't have much of a recollection), I tried to find her. The culprit must have been the chef, so off I went looking for the bastard except I didn't have any clothes on. I was totally starkers as I went through the hotel, knocking on every door and then staggering through the staff dormitory with everyone running for cover. I had made my mind up I was going to have a shag and nothing was going to stop me, I was shouting her name everywhere as loud as I could and expressing my intentions.

I woke up with the greatest of hangovers and a lump on my head where someone had obviously hit me with something to shut me up . . . and it worked. Whoever it was that hit me returned me to my bed and cleaned out all my cash. I wasn't game to have breakfast in the hotel for fear of ramifications, justifiably so. How in God's name could or would I ever explain my conduct?

'For fuck's sake, what in Jesus name did you get up to?' was Stef's opening words when we met for coffee. 'Have you gone mad or what?'

'Well, you told me to shag every old doll I could get my hands on and that's what I was trying to do, except I had a few too many drinks. But I must admit, it was fun trying and you were right, it helped me keep my mind off Serica.'

Of course, it goes without saying that that would be my last night at the Grand Hotel for many years to come.

It was during this period that I ran rampant and there was no shortage of women, single or married, willing to oblige a sweet-talking, young, sex-wild, cocky Corkie from Gurranabraher. Yes, sex was on every menu for entree, main course and desert. I'd like to say I was choosy but I wasn't and I more or less treated it as getting my own back on every woman—stupid yes, rational no. But then again, logic wasn't playing a very big part in my emotional life at that time. All I wanted to do was escape reality.

I was deeply hurting, I felt like I was drowning and the women were the straws I was grabbing at to keep me afloat until sanity returned. I was out of control when it came to women. I desperately needed comforting, reassurance and love. I wanted someone to hold and comfort me like a baby. I was looking for some logic in my crazy world and my only answer to it was to immerse myself in women and sex; as long as that was working, the pain of Marion and Serica and home didn't exist.

I'm not proud of this period of my life but then again you must remember this was a time before therapy became popular and, in any case, it was a time of hypocrisy in Ireland. And don't think for one moment any of the married women I spent time with sought coun-selling for their behaviour either. On the contrary, that's not what they were looking for and I can't recall any of them showing or stating any form of guilt, no, not even one.

And yet I know that I will be challenged many times in the future not only from my own but from the public-at-large and I wonder how many of those women will stand next to me and face the music. How many will sit back and say what I say: it was a time of secrets? Will they also cast stones at me, or will they, like me, break the cycle of lies and stand up and be counted? I'm sure I will receive many judgement days on this earth before I go to my almighty judge, and I will have to live with it, but I'm sure I will be standing alone for a long time before any of my married bed companions will put their hands up and join me. So, before you cast judgement, reflect for a moment—it's the people in glass houses who shouldn't throw stones.

CHAPTER SIX

A WAY OUT

DURING THIS TIME I befriended Clifford Davis. Clifford was about five years younger than me and was an extrovert like myself, who loved to party. Although he and I spent a fair bit of time together chasing women and drinking, we didn't have a lot else in common. In fact, we were like chalk and cheese. However, our lives would impact on each other.

It was he who drove me to Tralee to confront Serica in early April, 1974. It was my only attempt to reconcile with her and I froze at the sight of her as she entered The Old Brogue on the arm of another guy, looking her stunning best.

I never said a word and neither did she: dignity won the night as Clifford and I left to Charlie Rich asking me over the airwaves if I'd 'Happened to See the Most Beautiful Girl in the World'? Well I sure had, and I also felt like telling him he had shit timing, as if my heart wasn't broken enough.

I got Clifford a job working alongside me in sales and management. He had previously been a watch repairer. Being an extrovert and quick to pull a chick, I thought his talents were wasted behind a workbench, and my views were proven right.

I was summoned to Dublin to attend a meeting where I was introduced to a new member of the crew who would be working under me:
an Englishman named John Osborne, who I was to find out later,
arrived in Ireland from Australia via Africa. We worked very closely
over the next few months in between my regular bouts of drinking and
shagging, and I got lots of stories about Australia from John including
the one about when he was running a petrol station in Port Headland
in West Australia . . .

One morning he opened the mail to find there was a massive bill
from the tax man. Then and there he and his wife decided to catch a
plane that very day for South Africa rather than pay up. On arrival
in South Africa they bought a VW station wagon and filled the boot
with whiskey that they sold in Botswana. They then drove up and
across Africa through Europe to Ireland, hence he arrived here all
cashed up.

John was the first person I ever knew who had an American Express
card and it was he who in our short time together introduced me to
fine foods, good restaurants and top-class wines. He was also the one
who I first saw switch price tags on expensive wines when shopping.
He used to say the Irish wouldn't know a good bottle of wine if you hit
them over the head with it.

❋　❋　❋

Joe Rice left a message at the office for me to be at his place by seven.
I'm always punctual and Joe was at the door on my arrival. He told me
that his wife's sister, Ann, had a friend also called Ann, who was in the
lounge room. She had run away from her husband in Limerick and
she needed someone to take her out and cheer her up.

'Well, Joe, you got the right boy for the job. A few drinks down at the
Ardmaning, then a spin out on the road and a good shag in the back seat
and she won't have any problems.' Joe nodded, 'It's your call.'

I was taken by surprise when I finally met Ann, she was so pale and gently quiet. 'Would you like to come for a few drinks?' I asked. 'I'll get my coat,' was all the answer I wanted.

After four pints and two hours listening to her story of, 'He doesn't care any more and I love my two children,' I suggested we go for a drive. It didn't take long to find out she didn't care too much for him either as we both shagged ourselves stupid in the back of the car. No whingeing now, only groaning and fogged up windows and sweaty, smelly bodies.

Ann returned home to Limerick for the weekend to 'the husband who didn't care for her' and the 'two children she loved,' but before leaving she invited me to spend the following weekend in Limerick. I don't know why I accepted, but I did.

I arrived on Saturday at noon at her door to be greeted by 'the husband who didn't care for her' and I introduced myself as Joe's brother, as Ann and I had previously arranged. I was escorted into the kitchen where Ann and the 'two children she loved' were having dinner. Introductions to the children and pleasantries were swapped and I was asked to join in for dinner. I felt no guilt at all at the hypocrisy of it as I understood no love was lost between Ann and her husband. After dinner I excused myself and thanked them for their hospitality. They then invited me to spend Sunday afternoon with them.

After spending the evening at Durty Nelly's drinking, singing and chatting up Yanks, I woke early to a surprisingly bright Limerick morning. After breakfast and reading the Sunday papers, I felt a desperate need to write to Serica's mother and try to explain the reasons for my relationship, to hopefully make her feel not so ashamed of her daughter and, most of all, I hoped she would take the time to tell Serica that my intentions were rightful even if I did go about it in a selfish and stupid manner.

After finishing my eight page soul-searching letter, I set off to post it on my way to Ann. I then drove her and her husband to Ballybunion in County Kerry (where else?—the old Kerry magnet was always working). We stopped a couple of times for a few pints on the way there and back and while in Ballybunion we spent an hour on the beautiful beach. I reminisced about all the good times I had there. From the first night I spent in Bernie Callaghan's Cliff House Hotel, and the great nights I had in the Central Hotel and Horans.

I well remember one occasion when I was in Horans the previous summer. I was being the typical commercial traveller in my casual clothes. In Ireland at that time it was the trend that commercial travellers wore suits during the day and at night when we went pub crawling we would change into our casuals. Other workers went casual during the day and dressed up for the night out, so it was easy to pick the commercial travellers.

There I was, peering at the talent with my back to the bar, when this stunner beckoned me over. I tried to ignore her as I assumed she may be calling someone else. I sure wasn't the pick of the crop in Horans that night. She waved at me again twice and I turned and faced the bar. Then a tap on the shoulder.

'Hi, I'm Freda Wallace and I'm from Newry. Would you like to join us for a drink or are you shy?'

'No, I'm not shy and, yes, I'd love to join you. I didn't realise you were beckoning me.'

'What would you like?'

'No, it's my pleasure,' I assured her.

'You can have your pleasure later,' she replied, 'now, I'm buying.' I held up my almost finished pint of Double Diamond and said, 'Another.' She carried the drinks to her table, introduced me to her friends, threw back her drink, told me to do likewise and said, 'Let's get out of here.'

It was an absolutely beautiful night as we walked across the beach to where she had rented a caravan in the caravan park, located on the hill on the other side of the bay. We strolled, cuddled and kissed all the way.

'You really didn't want to stay, did you?' she said.

'You're kidding? And miss this? I may have a Cork accent but I'm not a fool.'

'You don't really want to stand here smooching against this caravan for the next hour or so, do you? How about you come in for a cup of tea?'

It sounded a lot better. Anything to get us closer to the bed.

Just as the kettle began to whistle, came the familiar comment, 'You don't really want a cup of tea do you?' Before she finished the sentence I was stripped and ready and she joined me in record time.

But before I jumped in the bed I said, 'For chrisakes why didn't you ask me first if I wanted to go to bed?'

'That wouldn't have been ladylike now would it?' She smiled.

I paused and scratched my head. 'But what are you doing now?'

'That's different. You would have thought I was cheap.'

'No no,' I groaned, 'I wouldn't have cared.' Then I thought for a second, *What am I saying?* 'You're right. I don't understand women's logic nor do I want to try, at least not now. For there's a job to be done.'

Next morning, the sun shone through the window to show me the full extent of Freda's beautiful half-exposed body. I may have had trouble in my younger days picking up an old doll, but wasn't having trouble any longer and I wasn't complaining . . . Still, I'd sure rather be waking up next to Serica in Tralee.

Freda's hand moved over to my starting button and I was back on top going like a bat out of hell. Whoopie! Afterwards, she asked me 'What are you doing today?'

I thought for a minute and then replied, 'Maybe we could go for a trip down the coast to Ballyheigue and back through Tralee and Listowel where we could drop into John B. Keans for a few drinks.

'No, no, the question was, "What are *you* doing today?", not "What are *we* doing today?"'

'I don't understand.'

'Yes, yes you do,' she grinned.

'Don't you want to spend the day with me?' I asked.

'Nope.'

'But what about last night and just now?'

'Fantastic, fabulous, brilliant, passionate—all that and more, but

91

my boyfriend is coming to join me today for the rest of the week.'

My mouth wouldn't close, I was in shock. 'You mean, you picked me up and used me?' I heard myself saying out loud.

'Yep,' she said. 'Don't tell me you never did that,' she added.

I was outraged. 'I didn't know girls did that, do they?' I asked.

'You better believe it.'

I felt a smile come on my face: 'Checkmate.'

I suppose the part that annoyed me the most was that no one would believe that a gorgeous chick picked me up and gave me a fabulous night and, of course, I wasn't going to tell anyone that she dumped me the next morning. But I must admit, every now and again, I get the giggles when I think of the brazen Freda Wallace from Newry.

Ann's husband asked me to stay over at their place for the night when we got back to Limerick, which I declined for fear of feeling too much of a hypocrite. I knew if I stayed I would have ended up in the marriage bed as soon as he went to work the next morning. So Ann arranged to meet me in Cork the following weekend.

Again I was going back to Cork. Cork of the troubles of my youth and the brewing problems of the future. I spent most of the week working with John and most of the nights drinking with Clifford discussing the opportunities and lifestyle of Australia.

The busy week flew, but I did again take time to write to Serica's mum and again I felt I ought to let her know that I didn't just write the last letter as an afterthought, but I sincerely meant every word I wrote and was truly sorry for the pain I caused, not only to her but all the family. Hopefully one day she might find a little forgiveness for me (not that I deserved it) and understand that I did truly love her daughter.

Ann gave me a reason to consider leaving Ireland. She told me she was definitely going to leave 'the husband who didn't care for her' and the 'two children she loved'. We spent the weekend trying to sort out the what-ifs and buts in the White Lady Hotel in the beautiful town of Kinsale. I would have to sell my car to raise the cash, and if we decided to go, there would be no turning back.

We agreed to think about it for a week and if we both felt the same way at the end of it we would then go to England in two weeks time. I had to consider if I were to go, what about Niall and Liz? What if I never saw them again? How would I cope without smelling Liz's baby smell, seeing Niall's loving innocent eyes, feeling their hugs and kisses? I may not be the best father God put on this earth but I had a responsibility. My mother and father stayed together through thick and thin even though many a time I wished they didn't because of the constant squabbling and tension. I had to consider how my children might be feeling with Mary and I causing the same tensions. In the future, would the children be saying the same thing I was saying now? *Oh, God, please help me.*

This decision was too much. So much hurt and pain would be caused, how would it affect Mum and Dad and Breda? And what about Aunt Mary? What would Stef think? I knew if I decided to go, a lot of people were going to be hurt and it wasn't going to last just for a day, it was going to be for a long, long time. It was crucial if I decided to go, I had better consider the consequences carefully and I knew the effects on some of my loved ones would be devastating.

If I went, I risked being caught and extradited back to Ireland and charged with deserting a marriage with children, an offence that would send me to prison. This meant I wouldn't be able to let the authorities know where I was for twelve years until the statute of limitations had expired because I sure as hell didn't want to ever spend even a day in prison. I certainly couldn't understand why I had to go to prison just because two people fell out of love.

This decision, right or wrong, was a cross I was going to have to carry for the rest of my life. I was going to have to be strong enough to carry it forever, and forever is a long time.

I did all the fatherly things for the next week hoping the cross would be taken from me. I even prayed I would die before decision time, but no saints came to assist me. I suppose it was a busy week for them, perhaps bigger problems than mine elsewhere got priority. Just like someone contemplating suicide, I began to leave hints and subtle comments to all those who I thought would be hurt by my going. I hadn't yet decided but subconsciously I was going through the motions of someone who had.

I couldn't figure out why I was deciding this—going with someone who I met a month ago and who I had nothing in common with. I felt the decision was now being made for me. What would be would be, and I was going with the flow, not knowing where it would take me. The puppet master was in control.

We agreed Monday week I would pick Ann up at her place in Limerick at 10 am, after she dropped the children off at school. Then we would head for London. I now had eight days to give and get as many kisses from the children as I possibly could. I hated what Ireland was making me do: self-exile for at the very least twelve years because if its prejudice. After all, if I was prepared to live my life and marriage as a sham I could stay. Ireland—once the land of saints and scholars— is now the land of hypocrites and sinners and I was leaving, and hating the thought of possibly never returning. Ireland deprived me of so much in my youth and yet I hated the thought of leaving.

Why me? Why did this have to happen to me? Was it because I fell in love with the right person at the wrong time, or was there a bigger agenda that God had written and I just didn't understand it? Well, whatever it was it sure was hurting like hell. If I'd previously thought being in love with Serica was hurtful, I was in for a rude awakening. Nothing would match the inner pain of not seeing Liz and Niall for twelve precious years.

My last week in Cork was heartbreaking.

Kissing my grandmother, Liz, holding her hand, knowing I'd never see her again was so difficult. I would always regret not telling Stef, who gave me so much understanding and love—a beautiful man who taught me so much and whom I'd admired so. My Aunt Mary (a living saint) I think knew in her heart it would be the last time we would kiss. 'Look after yourself, my son,' was all she said. But the words rang loud in my ears, 'Son, you may have been born in shit, but you don't have to live in it . . .' Hurt and pain was all around in everyone I saw and everything I did. It was a week of hell and all through it I had to try and sell my car to raise the necessary cash.

I found myself wandering the streets looking for all the places that meant something special to me. One of the most special was the Arcadia Ballroom, where we spent many Saturday and Sunday nights dancing. Saturday nights were fabulous, you needed a shoehorn to get in as the place was so packed. All the local favourites would play there: Brendan O'Brien; Joe Mc and The Dixies; Brendan Bowyer and The Royal Showband; The Clipper Carlton; Billy Brown and The Freshman; Dickie Rock and The Miami.

The support was usually Cork's own Dukes Showband with The Hendrick Brothers, Barry and Herbie, who used to do a brilliant rendition of the Everly Brothers' songs. Herbie gave me my first and only lesson on guitar, he was a great musician and a lovely person. I was inspired by his talent, he was a gifted person. I am forever grateful to him for his time and patience and, as money was scarce, of course, there was no cost for the lesson. Thank you, Herb.

Two of the other regular support bands were The Impact Showband, later to become The Fontana Showband, or was that vice versa? They had an inspiring young musician in their midst who soon shot to international stardom when he started his own threesome group called Taste. Rory Gallagher was then a very shy young man, a caterpillar just waiting to emerge into a beautiful butterfly.

It was well worth queuing up in the cold, rain-drenched, winter's nights. You usually had to queue for quite a while especially when the international stars played there, and there were many: The Everly Brothers; The Springfields; The Seekers; Brian Poole and The Tremeloes; Dave Dee; Dozy, Beaky, Mick and Tich; The Troggs, Chubby Checker; Jim Reeves; and The Searchers all strutted the stage there.

Sunday nights were usually reserved for introducing new Irish bands to Cork, so I got to see most of the emerging young Irish musicians. Us guys often hung around after the gig to give the bands an assessment of how they went on their first night in Cork and we strummed around on their guitars, all real casual stuff. Yes, sometimes, the thought of strumming a guitar with Clem Quinn from The Miami was more enticing than walking a girl home. Also, there weren't as many people who turned up to the Sunday night dance gigs as Saturday, so the bands weren't under as much pressure and, of course, that also meant there weren't as many girls at the event. But in fairness it must be said, in spite of comments from the likes of Bob Geldof, those bands worked hard for their money on stage, sometimes playing for three to four hours non-stop—none of this twenty-minutes on, twenty-minutes off malarky. They certainly earned their money in my view. And on many occasions they didn't receive their rightful portion of the monies taken as they were exploited by unscrupulous promoters.

Yeah, I stood there and recalled all the greats and had tears in my eyes.

I wandered over to the railway station, across from the 'Arc', and reminisced about the times my Aunt Eilie took me and her flock of seven to Youghal on the train in the summertime. And this was also where I paid a local truck driver one pound, ten shillings to teach me to drive in a CIE ten-tonne truck as an under-aged person, but who cared? It was cash money in my teacher's back pocket.

I walked up to the quays and stared at where all the Yankee coal and grain ships used to dock. I thought of the times I used to bring my father his dinner when he worked on those ships shovelling their contents into big buckets, and I would pinch as much coal as I could get into the empty dinner basket to bring home to keep us warm. Fathers never brought coal home, it was beneath them, but I was more worried about the cold than the loss of dignity.

I walked up the South Mall, passed The Assembly rooms, the old cinema that was now closed where we saw The Bowary Boys, Laurel and Hardy, and The Three Stooges all for three-pence each. My pals at the time used to call it the 'arse and belly' rooms because us kids didn't know what 'assembly' meant.

Aunt Mary, Breda and I—the pants were borrowed for the photograph

efore I started at the niversity of Life

Modelling a jumper Liza knitted for me

A rare photo of Mick
(dad) and I

IN
LOVING MEMORY
OF THE
NORTH INFIRMARY
HOSPITAL
Born 1774
Murdered 1987
By Government Cutbacks
Age 213 Years

R.I.P.

Sadly Missed By
Denis Lyons F.F. · Dan Wallace F.F.
Bernard Allen F.G. · Liam Burke F.G.
Maureen Quill P.D.
ALWAYS REMEMBERED AT ELECTION TIME

The North Infirmary Hospital
where I spent most of my
childhood and where aunt Mary
worked in the laundry for
almost forty years

RIGHT: A flyer demonstrating
the community backlash to
closing of the hospital in 1987

LEFT: Aunt Mary (my own angel)

The calm before the storm—wedding day, April Fools Day, 1967
The wedding group at the Church of the Assention

ABOVE: Cork Hibernians team, winners of the FAI cup in 1973
FROM LEFT TO RIGHT: John Brohan, Frankie Connolly, Carl Humphries, Declan O'Mahoney (goalie),
John Lawson, Sonny Sweeney, Dave Bacuzzi, Jerry Coyne, Dave Wiggington, Dinny Allen,
Noel O'Mahoney, Martin 'Fada' Sheehan. Picture courtesy of the *Irish Examiner*

The laneway (Cobbages Lane) off Shannon Street where Breda and I played during the day. At the archway on the right was the entry to 50 Shannon Street and an abundance of rats

Breda modelling the shawl that some women wore to conceal their pregnancies

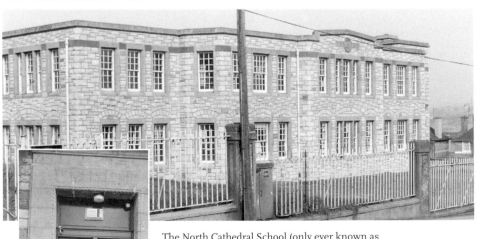

The North Cathedral School (only ever known as the 'new school') where they told me I would amount to nothing. They also told me I could not join the school band because I was tone deaf (glad to have proven them wrong)

LEFT: Revisiting my old school in 2003—it is now no longer a school

ABOVE: The Cork Opera House where I floated onto the world of music. Gurranabraher in the background

LEFT AND BELOW: Program from one of the shows signed by the cast 1968

SYNOPSIS OF SCENES:

ACT ONE —

Scene 1	Stage of Ford Theatre, Baltimore
Scene 2	Corridor (Back Stage)
Scene 3	The Dressing Rooms of Fred Graham & Lilli Vannessi
Scene 4	Padua
Scene 5	Street Scene, Padua
Scene 6	Backstage
Scene 7	Fred's & Lilli's Dressing Rooms
Scene 8	Before the Curtain
Scene 9	Extenoi Church

ACT TWO —

Scene 1	Theatre Alley
Scene 2	Before the Curtain
Scene 3	Petruchio's House
Scene 4	Corridor (Back Stage)
Scene 5	Fred's and Lilli's Dressing Rooms
Scene 6	Corridor (Back Stage)
Scene 7	Before the Asbestos Curtain
Scene 8	Baptista's House

DANCERS:— Misses Nuala McCann, Kathleen Murphy, Pauline Haughey, Katherine Murphy, Lucy Leonard, Norma Johnson, Ann Mulqueen, Mary Foley.

LADIES' CHORUS: Misses Marie Bruton, Mary Collins, Ann O'Callaghan, Phyllis Slyne, Olive Kidney, Theresa Fitzgerald, Ann Keating, Peg Murphy, Margaret Lyons, Rita Campion, Ann Kidney, Joan Kelly, Kay Lyne, Elizabeth Foran, Helen Dineen, Marie Dempsey

MEN'S CHORUS: Messrs. Larry O'Shea, Con Hurley, David Bradley, Ray Buckley, Frank O'Brien, Brian Walsh, Michael Bowen, Jim Mountjoy, Michael Condon, Noel Quinn, Declan Murphy, Eamonn Teehan, Sean Healy

The Society wishes to thank the following firms for their assistance in mounting the production:—
Messrs. Barry's, Auctioneers, Academy Street;
Messrs. C. O'Connell Ltd., Lavitt's Quay;
Messrs. Browne Thompson & Co., Academy Street;
Messrs. T. W. Murray & Co., Patrick Street.

Miss Jenkins' Hair in "The Taming of the Shrew" by Brian Peters, Wig Creations Ltd., London;
Flowers by Mrs. Millar, Flower Shop, Woodford Bourne;
Hair Styles by Henri Michael;
Telephones by the Department of Posts & Telegraphs

COMMITTEE OF THE CORK OPERATIC SOCIETY
President — Commander George Crosbie
Chairman — H. Fitzgerald-Smith, M.R.I.A.I.
Hon. Secretary — Miss Rosarii McNamara
Hon. Treasurer — Patrick Fleming
Miss Ann Reilly, Messrs. Larry O'Shea, Con Hurley, David Bradley, Ray Buckley

● VISIT THE BARS DURING THE INTERVAL AND AFTER THE SH

CORK OPERA HOUSE

COMMENCING TUESDAY, 26th NOVEMBER, 1968
Nightly at 8   ☎ 20022

GOLDEN JUBILEE PRESENTATION (1918 - 1968)
THE CORK OPERATIC SOCIETY presents
"KISS ME, KATE"
(by arrangement with N.O.D.A., London)
Music and Lyrics by Cole Porter
Book by Sam and Bella Spewack

THE CAST (in order of their appearance)

Fred Graham (actor, producer, writer)
Harry Trevor
Lois Lane   BARRY KENT
Ralph (stage manager)   Dan Donovan
Lilli Vannessi   Monica Murphy
Hattie   Noel Quinn
Stage Doorman   ANGELA JENKINS
Paul   Ann Reilly
Bill Calhoun   Sean Healy
First Man   Noel Murphy
Second Man   Jim Mountjoy
Harrison Howell   Pat Fenton
                                                 Frank Kelleher
                                                 Liam O'Connell
                                                 William Williams

"TAMING OF THE SHREW" Players
Bianco (Lois Lane)
Baptista (Harry Trevor)
Gremio (First Suitor)
Hortensio (Second Suitor)   Monica Murphy
Lucentio (Bill Calhoun)   Dan Donovan
Katharine (Lilli Vannessi)   Pat Fenton
Petruchio (Fred Graham)   Noel Egan, A.T.C.
                                                 Patrick Murray
                                                 ANGELA JENKINS
                                                 BARRY KENT

Production Directed by:
Guest Conductor   Del Donovan
Choreography   Richard Geary
Chorus Mistress: Rose Kearns
Decor and Lighting: Noel Egan, A.T.C.
Stage Manager: Patrick Murray
Assistant Stage Manager: H. Fitzgerald-Smith
Costumes: Melanie Fitzgerald-Smith
                                                 Derry O'Donovan, Dublin

THIS IS AN AMATEUR PRODUCTION

This is a list of pubs and eat out
joints along with the names
and address of my new house
mates. Bob Dallas (cab driver)
gave me this list in the foyer of
the Victoria Hotel—a life saver
when starting anew

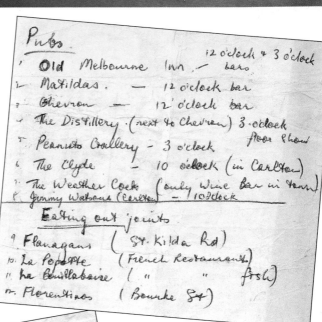

Pubs.
1. **Old** Melbourne Inn — 12 o'clock & 3 o'clock bars
2. Matildas. — 12 o'clock bar
3. Chevron — 12 o'clock bar
4. The Distillery (next to Chevron) 3 o'clock
5. Peanuts Gallery — 3 o'clock floor show
6. The Clyde — 10 o'clock (in Carlton)
7. The Weather Cock (only wine bar in town)
8. Jimmy Watsons (Carlton) — 10 o'clock

Eating out joints.

9. Flanagans (St. Kilda Rd)
10. La Popotte (French Restaurant)
11. La Bouillabaise (" " fish)
12. Florentinos (Bourke St)

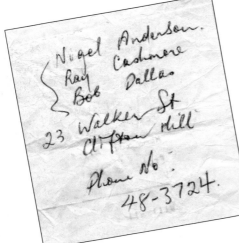

Nigel Anderson.
Ray Cashmore
Bob Dallas
23 Walker St
Clifton Hill

Phone No.
48-3724.

Getting a suntan outside the batchelor pad in Bendigo Street, Elwood

At my desk in Mazda Motors with a picture of Elizabeth in the background

My prize for being top salesman—I got to drive David Syer's (the manager) magnificent Austin Healy

Mick and Liza at the Shrine of Remembrance on their visit to Melbourne

Jonathan and Emmett, checking out the mode of local transport in County Clare

BELOW RIGHT: No longer in exile—Emmett, Jonathan and one of my favourite pubs, Durty Nellys, on the Ennis road out of Limerick

BELOW: Kissing the Blarney Stone

ALL ABOVE: Sharing with Jonathan my favourite place on earth, DunCaoin Slay Head, County Kerry, the setting for *Ryan's Daughter*— a writer's paradise, where I wrote most of *A Time of Secrets* and other works

Breda and Dr Maurice Hickey (the wonderful surgeon who saved my life) at the launch of *Window To My Soul* & *Straight From The Heart* at Murphys-Heineken in 1989

The Arcadia (the Arc, the nucleus of cork entertainment in the 60s)
—demolished to build units

Dubliner Fran Meen
performing my entry in
song for Euro 1990 'Say
That You Love Me'

BOVE: In the Green Room before the show

IGHT: Mixing it with my peers Tommy
nd Jimmy Swarbrigg, Ireland's premier
ongwriters, after the show

Mitchell's Ave, Tralee

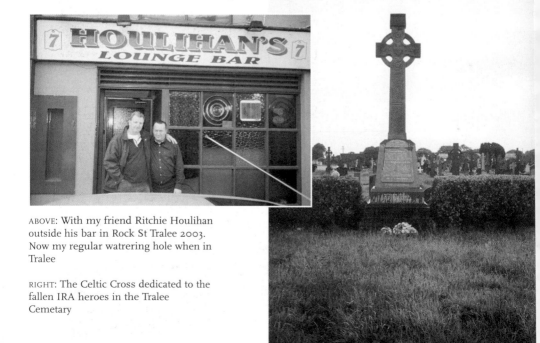

ABOVE: With my friend Ritchie Houlihan outside his bar in Rock St Tralee 2003. Now my regular watrering hole when in Tralee

RIGHT: The Celtic Cross dedicated to the fallen IRA heroes in the Tralee Cemetary

ABOVE: With Johnny Logan, two Irish Aussies in Oslo, 1996

RIGHT: Another Aussie, Gina G ('Just A Little Bit') representing UK, Oslo 1996

ABOVE: Eurovision 1995, in Dublin with my friend and business partner Allan Sherratt

RIGHT: Ireland's ESC winner Eimear Quinn (The Voice), Oslo 1996

TOP: Emmett and I doing what we love most, jamming it up on Sunday mornings

ABOVE: My good mate Peter Williams, ex-lead singer of The Mixtures ('The Push Bike Song') relaxing at home in Australia, posing as musos do

ABOVE RIGHT: Samantha O'Carroll, Cork's newest Everest conquerer

RIGHT: Georgie Furey, my very good friend, and I after a gig at the Melbourne Concert Hall

I stood outside The Stardust Club and again began to reminisce about the music, and all the great nights I had there. I moved on up The Grand Parade till I came to the corner of Washington Street where I looked left to where I got my first job in Dwyers as a twelve-and-a-half-year-old boy, on one pound, eight shillings per week. Dwyers was both a sad and glad experience for me. Sad because I was ridiculed by some of my elderly work colleagues due to my dyslexia and my appearance. Basically, I didn't have any decent clothes because they were all were second-hand from the coal quay (a local market) that my mother bought for a few pence rather than pay shillings or pounds at a regular store.

Even my scout shirt I wore for the eighth Cork Boy Scouts was a Girl Guides gym slip, cut down at the waist—and badly at that—so bad in fact, I used to wait until no one was looking to take it off when we were on hiking trips on hot summer days. To make matters worse, it was dyed blue, so every time it rained on the hiking trips, the colour ran and, guess what? I felt like the first incredible hulk, only a blue one, minus the muscles. My shoes matched my socks well. Very religious, very 'holey'! The only things intact were my trousers and belts. Everything else was well worn and second or third-hand. The uniform may have been a worn hand-me-down, but I kept it spic-and-span, and I wore it with enormous pride for many years as the leader of the fox patrol.

However, I let all the snide remarks from those under-educated, middle class, up themselves wankers pass over my head. I was too streetwise to be intimidated by them. Then there was the wonderful experience of working with great lads who had treasure chests for hearts and were so understanding: Cal McCarthy, Noel Hurley, the very athletic Bobby Fitzgerald and Alfie Mansfield. I learned more from those people than I did from my teachers, and it was while I used to vacuum the offices of the Dwyers Brothers that I fell in love with the game of rugby. I would look at the rugby match programs on their desks and be in awe of the thought of going to Lansdown Road to see Ireland play Wales and all the other rugby nations.

I couldn't afford a lolly at the time as the full one pound eight shillings wages went to Liza for food and I got one shilling back for pocket money to go to the pictures. It's not that I wanted any more, because I understood Liza needed it to put food on the table. Breda was in hospital with rheumatic fever in her heart at the time and I was the sole provider as Mick's money was for his drink.

Alfie Mansfield was one of three local delivery van drivers and a wonderful old soul of a man. He, like myself, only had one lung so he took it upon himself to look after me and on many occasions he gave me his own lunch when I didn't have any. He had a lovely nurturing quality about him and while I don't think I ever thanked him enough I'm sure he's reading my mind now as, sadly, he passed away some time ago.

Right across the road from Dwyers was P.D. Sayers where I worked as a very streetwise kid at the ripe old age of sixteen. That was where I met Stef, who I liked straight away, who became the brother I never had and my mentor. I was in shock when one of my work colleagues told me Stef was Protestant. Being educated in the very biased Catholic south of Ireland, we were told to avoid almost everything and anything that didn't think or act like a Catholic. So when Stef looked and acted like a Catholic, I was confused. I suppose I thought he would try to convert me, or something. I wasn't prepared for the most lovely-mannered, good-humoured and quick-witted person I would ever meet.

God only knows what I had expected a Protestant to be, but it didn't resemble Stef. It now shames me to think I was so narrow-minded. He had the most generous heart and kind nature and all this he shared with me, the kid from Gurranabraher. He gave me so much time, help and understanding without ever questioning the cost. To say I was furious when our local priest refused me permission to attend Stef's father's funeral was an understatement. I spent the funniest night of my life with his mother and all his family at the wake—a real bonding time—and the following day I proudly shouldered his father's coffin with my very dear and close friend. I was willing to be excommunicated by the Church at the time for doing so.

I understood little of the enormous prejudice the Protestants underwent in Cork, ostracised as they were by the Catholic majority. Or should I say that us Catholics had our minds poisoned by the clergy, a sense of hate was taught to us about Protestants. Religion is about loving your neighbour and sharing, so to this day I can't figure out why we were taught as kids to hate those who never did anything to us, other than praise their God in a church that wasn't ours.

We all shared the same city air, rain and cold. Why was their prejudice forced upon us children in school and church? No wonder we had secrets and problems in Ireland, it was the fears and the prejudices of our clergy that were instilled in us as children. The segregation in Cork was not of our own making and no doubt that pattern was widespread in the south of Ireland, a reverse situation of the problem in Northern Ireland.

The Church had far too much influence in politics and because of this it ruined many a life, sadly, in the name of God. It took the high ground on moral issues where it lacked within. They forgot the basic fundamental principle of leading by example, to 'do as I say, but not as I do' . . .

I stood outside the 7UP bar where I had my very first bottle of Phoenix beer with my old school mate, Doc Doherty. Across the road from the 7UP is The Capital Cinema where I saw Elvis in *G.I. Blues* and *Blue Hawaii*. I strode up to the corner where the Roundy House stood to view the coal quay from where almost all of my childhood clothes came from. I knew all the hawkers as my mother regularly gossiped with them with me on her arm when we went into town.

I walked past Guys, Everleys and The Pavilion Cinema on Patrick Street, till I came to Academy Street, which I turned into and I walked past *The Cork Examiner* to view The Cork Opera House at the end of the street, on the river front, for the last time. I had performed there many times with The Cork Operatic Society.

The wonderful musical, *The Bell of New York*, was my hands-on introduction to the musical world, thanks to The Cork Operatic Society and Larry O'Shea. This was my first real look into the mechanics, the staging and workings of a theatre show. I was gob-struck with everything about the theatre. First of all, I was embarrassed because of my background and I didn't have a lot of self-confidence about my singing voice. Larry was an enormous help to me in overcoming my inhibitions. He used to tell me how exciting it was for him just watching me, sapping up all the energy of the show. Me and my inquisitive nose for knowledge to learn as much as I could.

I loved every aspect of the business. Every time I turned up to rehearsals I got goose pimples, I was in my seventh heaven. Everyone accepted me warmly, but that still didn't stop me from feeling out of place. I kept asking myself, what was someone like me, with my background of a drunken father, from rat-infested dwellings, doing in now middle-class Cork? Maybe if they found out my background they might not want me there, hence I felt I was the keeper of secrets again and I felt I could never get away from them. In spite of this, I refused to give in to my concerns and Aunt Mary's words would always be there to reassure me, 'You may be born in shit, but you don't have to live in it . . .'

And so I took my first step onto the world stage in The Cork Opera House which, if my memory serves me correctly, was in November, 1967. Actually, my description wasn't quite right when I said I stepped onto the world stage, it was more like I floated onto the stage. I had goose pimples on goose pimples with excitement. No nerves, not even a twinge. I was sharp, confident and cocky and the one sad note of the night was neither Liza nor Mick turned up to see their son doing them proud. The three years I spent with the society would become an enormous benefit to me later on in life, but for now, I loved every minute of it.

We had some really funny times there also. Once, when between acts during the staging of 'The Taming of the Shrew', my dresser was doing up the buttons of my costume jacket and I was preoccupied reading the production directions by Dan Donovan. Dan was shouting for us to get ready for cue and in the haste of things I was just about to step on stage when someone grabbed hold of my jacket and pulled me back, rather firmly. Attached to the other end of my jacket was a very concerned Dan Donovan. 'Were you going to go on stage in only your underpants and your jacket?' he enquired, to my amazement. In the midst of all the rush of changing of costumes, I had forgotten to put on my leotards. I'm sure had Dan Donovan not been on hand to keep an eye on his charge that night the mood of the show would have quickly moved from a musical to a comedy! And God knows what that might have done to my confidence and my ego, surely not a lot. I used to feel really proud when on many occasions I would hear members of the audience comment, 'Oh, Jesus, is that Liza's son?' and I would respond by winking back, giving them an extra thrill.

The after-parties were real eye openers, usually held in the tennis club on the Cork side of Cobh. Middle-class Cork didn't behave any differently to the rest of us after an abundance of alcohol, and the springs of my Mini Minor were never the same after those events. I can't imagine for one moment that I was the only lucky guy at those after-parties, and I'm sure I wasn't.

I am forever grateful to The Cork Operatic Society for the knowledge and opportunity it gave me to pursue my passion for music, for I gained a deeper understanding of all aspects of theatre. It was a magnificent opportunity for a young kid from the wrong side of the tracks to gain a further education at no cost. For all this, I thank you. I may have been just another member of the troop but it had a huge impact on my life and, believe it or not, it was the first ripple that would travel further and have a much greater impact on the major stage of European music.

Sadly, now, Larry O'Shea has passed away and I sometimes wish he were here to see the results of the seeds he sowed in that young enthusiastic kid. And yet, sometimes when I'm working in a music studio, I swear I can still hear his wonderful voice singing along with me . . . or maybe it's just wishful thinking . . . Larry, are you really standing by me? I hope so.

As I stood looking up at The Opera House and thought of all the fun nights I'd had there with Larry and all the crew I thought, *How could I hate Cork?* And in my heart of hearts, I knew I didn't, I was only looking for someone, or something, to blame. I was way, way too immature to have taken on the responsibilities of married life. I came from a dysfunctional family and I brought all the garbage of that with me.

Nothing in school, for the little time I spent there, prepared me for the real world. I had no proper life skills. Life was a mystery. All I knew was I just wanted to be loved and wanted by someone, and the women and the affairs filled that gap. All, except Serica and Marion.

It started to rain and I was grateful as it helped disguise my tears and there was a constant flow of faces passing by. I looked back at the Savoy Cinema where I had seen The Rolling Stones play. It was the week 'Little Red Rooster' hit number one in the charts. Boy-oh-boy, was that group an eye-opener! Such a vibrant bunch of musicians and with an outrageous Mick Jagger fronting. Yes, the original five were present, including Brian Jones.

Standing on the corner of Patrick Street and Lavitts Quay I looked up at the Church of the Ascension where I took my marriage vows, which now looked down apon me from the top of Cathedral Road and I sadly bowed my head as if to try to hide my guilt. Maybe if I didn't look up at it, Jesus wouldn't know what my plans were and he would ignore me and let me get on with my runaway scheme.

I walked briskly over Patrick's Bridge and down MacCurtin Street towards my car, parked by the Arcadia Ballroom, crying all the way, and hoping to God that no one else would have to go through such feelings of lonesomeness and isolation. So many faces around and yet I felt as if I was the only person walking the earth. It was as if Butch Moore, who sang Ireland's first entry in the Eurovision song contest, 'Walking the Streets in the Rain' was singing just for me: 'Nobody knows that I'm crying because I'm walking the streets in the rain . . .'

St. Martins Pools reminded me of Peter, a friend of mine who was their only rep, and what a character he was, one funny bloke. I remember asking him once over a few drinks, 'Why don't you have a girlfriend?' Peter's reply was, 'They're too bloody expensive, boy, and not worth it 'cos I'd sooner drink the money and enjoy it. Then I can get a brasser (prostitute) to shag every Friday night for a pound. Now isn't that better than spending a fortune on a bird and still not getting what I want? At least when I see a brasser I'm guaranteed a shag.

Come here and I'll tell you,' he whispered in my ear. 'Last week, my usual brasser was slapping me on the arse while I was riding her and she was shouting, "Come on, Peter. Come on," and I said to her, "Why do I have to come first? Am I riding in the Grand National or what?"' He giggled. 'I came second and it was a half hour later. No boy, no girlfriend for me. I get all I want for one pound and I know it's guaranteed, so why should I bother?' He had no argument from me.

I had one last night with Joe Rice and Clifford on the beer and never mentioned a word of my plans. I decided to tell John, my new assistant, of my intentions and he offered to drive me to Limerick to pick up Ann and then on to Dublin to catch a flight to London. I also organised to sell my car, for now I was down to two days left in Cork.

Saturday was split between the children and Stef, and I was hoping he might see something in my manner to give him a hint of what was about to happen and then he might persuade me to stay. I didn't have the heart to tell him, and so it was left to be.

On Sunday, I took Niall to Mass in the Ascension. Afterwards we walked down to Shandon Street to The Old Reliable, my father's favourite bar. I don't know what made me start, but I found myself explaining every detail of my future plans to Niall. I suppose I didn't want to leave and not let him know that I was doing it for everyone's interest, not mine alone, and hopefully I would never regret it and he would understand.

He kept asking me, 'Why are you crying?' I told him it was the wind that was causing it. Thank God he didn't ask me why the wind didn't make him cry for I wouldn't have had an answer. His hands felt so soft and his skin so pure and clear. He had a killer of a smile and he was breaking my heart with every 'Why Dad? Why?'

How do you answer a five-year-old?

I told him, 'I don't know, but it feels like the right thing to do, son. Only the future will tell if it was right or wrong and God must have other plans for me otherwise he would have asked me to stay. So it must be.'

We never got to The Old Reliable as we were too preoccupied. We walked and talked for three hours. I wanted to answer truthfully, from the heart, everything he asked me. I wanted him to know how I felt even though he kept saying, 'Why? Why?' And every time I gave an answer, I got 'Why?' again.

I was feeling downright lousy by now. You name it, I had it: guilt, shame, anger, frustration, loss and isolation. We called in to see Mum and Dad as I wanted to feel, touch and kiss them for what might be the last time. Twelve years is a long time to be exiled and God knows what might happen in between.

'The poor child is frozen,' Mum said when we arrived. Niall pulled back and hid behind my legs. The sight of a glass of lemonade and a two-shilling piece soon relieved him of his shyness.

She surveyed my dishevelled appearance. 'You look awful,' she said. She looked up and down the street. 'Where's your car?'

I lied that the car had an electrical fault, that it wouldn't start and was being repaired in Limerick so I was picking it up tomorrow (the same story I told Mary). The red eyes, I said, were due to an allergy. We didn't stay long because I knew they would be suspicious and I really didn't want to lie any more. Mum kissed me and held me and I wanted to be two years old again so she could comfort me and take away all of my pain. Dad just hugged me and I had a feeling he knew in his heart I was going because he normally didn't hold me.

Niall and I walked out the door but I left my heart behind and I daren't look back for I was crying again and I didn't want them to see.

Niall squeezed my hand to tell me Nan and Pop were waving.

While Mary was visiting some friends in the afternoon I took the opportunity to explain my story to Elizabeth in spite of her infancy, because I wanted her to hear it from me. I felt sure she would get lots of different versions in the future, but she heard it first and truthfully from me. I held her for ages and smelled the fabulous baby smell and thought, *Oh God, am I mad or what to be giving up this wonderful gift of fatherhood?*

But deep inside I knew it had to be. The puppet master was now pulling the strings and I felt I was no longer in control of my destiny. I was meant to be elsewhere—I wasn't sure where yet, but I knew it certainly wasn't here.

Let's see which way the wind blows.

CHAPTER SEVEN

NO TURNING BACK

JOHN OSBORNE AND his wife picked me up at 7 am to drive me to Limerick, but not before I tried to get my fill of kisses and hugs from Niall and Liz to last me twelve years. I was leaving home for the last time.

John kindly offered to hold onto what monies I had so I wouldn't lose them. He obviously confused my Irish accent with being stupid. I thanked him for his overwhelming generosity and assured him there was nothing worth his while holding onto. My only case held all my worldly possessions: one suit, one pair of shoes, four shirts, four underpants, four pairs of socks, two ties, one belt, one pair of football boots (God knows why I brought football boots instead of other essentials), a shaver and 50 soccer programs of various English clubs (including my most prized one, the 1978 Manchester United vs. Benfica European Cup final). Somehow I felt bringing the programs with me would help with the homesickness.

John stopped in Mallow for me to post another apologetic letter I had written the previous night to Serica's mum, again hoping that writing it might cleanse my soul a little.

It only took a minute to put Ann and her belongings in the VW station wagon. We wanted to get going out of Limerick as quick as possible for fear of being spotted. Ann told us she dropped the children off to school and had organised for someone to pick them up afterwards. Her husband would be home for dinner and he would look after them.

John drove like the wind to get us to the airport. We used false names on our airline tickets to London because it wasn't necessary to produce a passport flying from Ireland to England. The hour-and-a-half wait seemed like an eternity. When the time finally arrived to depart I was so relieved; paranoia was setting in. I was beginning to think that everyone who looked at me was a plainclothes policeman or woman. I was also very conscious of not telling John and his wife where we would be staying in London or where we might go from there for I felt they might tell. I figured if I gave them no information, then they had nothing to tell other than we went to London under assumed names. I didn't even tell them what the names were. I thanked him and his wife for being so helpful and gave him enough money to cover his petrol and time, and to have a good dinner on me at Arbutis Lodge in Cork and think kind thoughts of me.

The reality of self-exile hit me like a Muhammad Ali knockout punch. Not a good time to be having second thoughts, but nonetheless scary, very scary. I was angry and confused. Angry because Ireland was too narrow-minded to be able to cater for people like me, who came from a dysfunctional family and a failed marriage. Confused because I also knew Ireland had its ways of making allowances for the privileged and hypocrites.

I stood there counting down my last minutes on Irish soil begrudging all those I was leaving behind. A river of emotion flowed inside me as I tried very hard to contain the tears. In that moment, for the first time, I realised how much I really loved my Ireland. And I vowed to myself, *No way will I ever come back here a failure for if I'm to have this much pain I'm going to put it to good use and prove Aunt Mary right.*

Tears finally flowed as the plane rose from the tarmac into the sky. I strained to catch the very last glimpse of Ireland from my window as it disappeared into the distance.

On arrival in London we booked into the Tara Hotel. Our plan was to stay for about a week until we finalised where we would go to from there. We unpacked and went for a walk. Then in the evening we decided to go and see 'Hair', the stage show. We both could not sleep; Ann was crying and I was crying. We were both very upset over our respective children and comforted one another as brother and sister, rather than lovers. Sex was the last thing on our minds. We agreed under no circumstances would we make any phone calls for fear they may be traced back to the hotel.

The next day I hired a Ford Capri so that we could do some sight-seeing and hopefully take our minds off our worries. After driving around London seeing the usual tourist sights, we had dinner at a small eatery on Shaftesbury Street and later went to the movies to see 'The Exorcist'. This was not a smart idea for two Irish Catholics. Whatever hope we had of sleeping was gone as we were both con-vinced we would have a visit from The Devil. After two nights we both looked like we had gone fifteen rounds with Sonny Liston, red-eyed and stuffed.

On the third night, after a decent feed of fish and chips, we went to see an Australian movie, the sex-comedy, 'Alvin Purple'. The next morning we decided we should go to check on the requirements to get into Australia, and we headed off to Australia House on The Strand.

We were informed that there was no extradition treaty with Ireland and all we needed was a valid passport (so no visa required) and a chest x-ray to show we didn't have tuberculosis. The hospital in Charing Cross would do the x-rays and they also would have doctors on hand to do a medical to support the x-rays, whatever the result. No sooner said than done. We would pick up both x-rays and results the next day.

We shopped in the afternoon and returned to the hotel at 5 pm with bags in hand. As we entered the foyer all I could think of was, *Holy fuck, I don't believe it*. Standing in the centre of the foyer was the 'husband who didn't care for her'. After the initial shock, a million thoughts ran through my mind: *How did he know? Does he have the police with him? Does he have a gun? Who else is with him? Do I run or do I fight? I'm no coward and never was, so I'm not running.* I walked straight up to him and said, 'I suppose you want to talk to me,' and expected to be knifed. But to my amazement he replied, 'I want to talk to my wife and take her home.' I brazenly announced, 'In that case, you don't mind if I just say goodbye to her? And by the way, we didn't have sex here.'

I bid my farewell to Ann and the husband who did care for her, after all. Then I packed my bag in record time and payed my hotel bill plus an extra night for the newly reunited couple.

I sped off to the Londonderry Hotel in Park Lane, still mystified, not knowing how he knew where to find us. I guess it didn't matter in the end except I felt more than ever before the urgency to get out of England as soon as I could. I spent the night scouring the map of the world looking for a safe haven. Maybe Australia was not a good idea any more, I wasn't sure.

It's funny how small the world looks when you're looking for somewhere to hide. Which countries don't have an extradition treaty with Ireland? Who speaks English? Who doesn't require visas? I worked it down to three: South Africa, Canada and Australia. And I assumed a clear x-ray and medical was my 'in' to Canada and South Africa as well.

I spent the night writing letters, first to Serica's mother, again apologising and begging for her forgiveness, then to Mum and Dad, and Mary and those close to me. By daybreak I was an emotional wreck.

I checked out of the hotel without breakfast and headed for the hospital in Charing Cross for my x-rays and results. 'All clear' and I was on my way again. Next, I dropped off the hired car, only to be told, 'You can't hand it back until the week is up.'

'If you don't sort it out now you'll be picking it out of the River Thames later on today,' I replied.

'No problem, sir,' came back quickly.

I caught a cab to the British Airways office. I walked in and looked up at a huge map of the world on the wall. A young girl in a uniform asked if she could help me. 'Just give me a minute please,' I replied. I had to make a quick decision, so I made up my mind on the spot.

'May I have a ticket to Australia?'

'Return, sir?'

'No, one way, please.'

'Where to in Australia, sir?'

'Just Australia.'

'Yes, sir, but where in Australia?'

'Oh, hell, I don't know.' Then, *Oh yes, of course, Ronnie Dalany had luck there when he won a gold medal for Ireland in the one-mile run at the Melbourne Cricket Ground in the 1956 Olympics. Why not? It may also be lucky for me.*

'To Melbourne, Miss.'

'When would you like to go?'

'When is the next plane leaving?'

'There's one going through America at two o'clock and one going through Asia at seven. But the one going through America takes much longer.'

'If that's the first, I'll take it.'

With a look of astonishment on her face, I paid for my ticket and started to walk to the door. She called after me, 'Excuse me, sir. It's not normal that someone comes in here and buys a ticket to the other side of the world in such a casual manner. Can I ask you why?'

I turned sideways and smiled. 'Sure, I believe there's a doctor there who mends broken hearts and I've got a job for him. A real tough job.'

She looked at me sadly and muttered, 'It's a long way to go with your sorrows, Mister.'

'It's the end of the earth, isn't it?' I left tugging all my worldly possessions behind me in my tattered suitcase.

I hailed a taxi to the airport and told the driver if he got me there in record time there was a twenty-pound tip in it for him. No arguments.

I arrived a half-hour before check-in time, which was a relief. Then, *I'll have my last pint of Guinness for old time's sake.*

I no sooner took the glass from my mouth than the realisation of what was happening hit me. I looked at the boarding pass. *Oh my God, this is not a dream. It's real. Twelve years of exile, it's such a long time.* I thought of Jesus in the Garden of Gethsemane asking his father to take the chalice from him. I was hoping and asking the same. I was waiting to wake up from the nightmare, I wanted to be in my mother's arms, having her comfort me and tell me everything will be alright, that it was just a bad dream and when I grew up to be a big strong man I would be able to cope with whatever came my way. And here I was, a big strong man and falling apart at the seams, thinking of the isolation of twelve years in Australia, on the other side of the world, and knowing virtually nothing about the place other than the scraps of information John told me and that Ronnie Dalany won a gold medal in the 1956 Olympics. How smart is that? I certainly wouldn't get a certificate for research on my subject.

In the midst of my panic, my Aunt Mary came into my thoughts, reminding me that I was a very bright person and the world was my oyster and I could do anything and be whoever I wanted to be. 'If no one believes in you, always remember I do, and don't you ever forget it.'

I finished my pint, wiped my eyes dry and stood tall. I walked proudly to the loading gate to face my destiny in Australia knowing that no matter what happened I would always have the support and— more importantly—the love of Aunt Mary, the one person who loved me unconditionally.

CHAPTER EIGHT

EXILE

OUR ROUTE TO Australia was through New York, Los Angeles, Hawaii, Fiji, New Zealand, Sydney and finally, Melbourne. It was a very tiresome and relatively uneventful trip, with the exception of the customs officer I happened to come across in New York who was Irish and who went to great lengths to try to persuade me to stay in New York.

'I'll get you a job here, no problems. For Jaysus sake, what are you doing going to the end of the world for? You'd be better off here amongst your own and we would never see you short. What do you say?'

'It's too complicated,' I insisted, 'but thank you so much for your kindness.' We parted with him shouting after me, 'If you change your mind, you know where I am.'

On July 5, the day before my birthday, I saw from the sky what would be my new home for the next twelve years, at the least. I didn't know what to make of Melbourne, it was overcast and raining. I couldn't believe it, I was expecting tropical sunshine. After all, I was in Australia, not Cork or Dublin. I never heard anyone ever talk of rain in Australia. Maybe the pilot made a mistake or the crew forgot to wake me while I was sleeping and we were back in New Zealand. 'No no,' the hostess assured me, 'that's definitely Melbourne.'

No gangway so it was down the steps in the pouring rain and I ran across the tarmac towards the shelter of customs. Drenched and cold, I looked up at the grey rain-filled clouds. Surely the hostess had made a mistake!

'G'day, mate,' was the greeting as soon as I stepped inside. I thought, *What sort of asylum let this poor bastard out because no one told him it's pouring rain outside. Obviously he's not the full quid.*

I shook myself like a dog to get rid of the water from my rain-soaked clothes. The customs officer greeted me with another 'G'day' and I thought, *He's obviously from the same asylum as the first chap.* Couldn't he see I was soaking wet?

'Are you visiting?'

'No sir, I'm staying.'

'Do you have an x-ray to prove you don't have tuberculosis?'

'Yes, sir, I do.'

One minute later I was accepted to my new home, Melbourne.

Strange isn't it? I'm at the end of the world and I'm not falling off, I thought as I staggered to the taxi rank delirious with fatigue. Again I was treated to another 'G'day, mate.'

What's wrong with these people, how can they be so happy when it's buck-eting down? I was so exhausted from my trip the friendliness of the Australians made me feel even more alone. I wanted to blurt out, 'I'm not your mate, how could I be? Didn't you just see me arrive and how could I be your mate when you don't even know me?' Of course, now I am forever grateful for the wonderfully optimistic reception I received. It was a sign of the generosity of spirit that I was to benefit from on countless occasions over the years.

The taxi driver stood at the his door shouting to me as I struggled to put my worldly possessions in the boot, 'She'll be right, mate'. I looked around to see who 'she' was as he repeated himself, 'She'll be right, mate.' *I thought coming to Australia was going to make life a bit easier because they speak English. Maybe I got it wrong. I thought the Aborigines were black, but perhaps they are white . . .*

The driver eventually realised I had no idea what he was saying and joined in the loading of the boot.

'Where to, mate?'

'Can you take me to the most central hotel in the city, please?'

'Sure, the Victoria Hotel in Little Collins Street.' Pause. 'You Irish, mate?'

What a stupid question! I thought grumpily as I sat in the back seat, wet and chilled to the bone.

'No, I'm French. I'm just minding the accent for a friend of mine who's in jail for a while,' I joked. After his outburst of laughter he barraged me with questions:

'First time here, mate?'

'Yes.'

'Are you on holidays, mate?'

'No.'

'Are you staying, mate?'

'Yes.'

'Do you have relatives here, mate?'

'No.'

'Do you have a job, mate?'

'No.'

'What the fuck you doing here then, mate?'

'I migrated.'

His quick response was, 'And you know jackshit about the place?'

'That's right, mate.'

'So, all on your own then, mate?'

'Yes, mate.'

'I suppose it's a stupid question to ask an Irishman, but would you like to come for a drink with me and my mates as soon as you book into your hotel? Oh, and by the way, my name's Bob. Bob Dallas.'

'Bob, I'm Mike. Mike Bowen and, yes, it's a stupid question. I've never known an Irishman to knock back an offer for a drink.'

No 'She'll be right, mate' this time as we emptied the boot. Bob helped me with my cases to the room.

'Jesus, mate, you couldn't swing a dead cat in here. You'll have to do whatever rooting you're going to do standing up. Hardly room to lie down. Now the porter told me the nearest bank was next door so I'll pick you up in an hour after you unpack and do your banking. See you then, mate.'

'Thanks, mate.'

The hour was sufficient for me to do my chores.

The first thing to leave a mark on me about Melbourne was its distinct smell. Not pollution, just a very unusual smell. I couldn't put my finger on it and to this day I never found out what it was.

On our way to the John Curtin Hotel in Lygon Street, Bob explained that along with his taxi driving he was a part-time student at Royal Melbourne Institute of Technology studying sociology and that we were meeting his student mates at the pub. Bob did the introductions. 'Mike, this is Nigel, Don, John, Paul and Doug. To this very day, the events of ordering my first drink in Australia crack me up.

'What are you having, mate?'

'A pint,' I replied. 'Beer.'

Don put a large jug on the table and a load of small glasses. I assumed the glasses were for wine and assumed it was coming later. So I proceeded to drink from the jug, or what looked like a 'pint plus' to me, but the over-sized drink wasn't going to put my nose out of joint. After gulping down about a quarter of the jug, I found my new mates looking at me in disbelief.

'What?' I asked the group.

Nigel politely said, 'Did you want to drink the whole jug yourself?'

'Oops, do you mean this was meant to be shared out in those tiny little glasses? You're joking! No one in Ireland ever shares his pint with anyone. You mean you guys all drink out of those tiny, tiny glasses?' No macho guy in Ireland would be seen dead drinking out of anything less than a pint glass unless he was a poof. *Oh fuck. Lord, please don't tell me they're all gay.*

'Why don't I just buy a couple of extra jugs to make up for the extra that I will be drinking?' to which everyone agreed.

After a long day's drinking with my new mates, Bob suggested we should go to the Celtic Club and round the day off with some Guinness.

On arrival I introduced myself to the manager, who in turn introduced me to the president of the club, who, to my amazement at the time, didn't speak a word of Gaelic. In my drunken splutter I mumbled, 'You must be joking, not a word of Irish. Shit. That's like the Pope not being able to recite the "Our Father".' Bob hurried me away and back to my new mates and another pint of Guinness.

We all finally retired to my tiny room in the Victoria Hotel to polish off my only two bottles of duty-free Grand Marnier and watch the men's singles Wimbledon final between the local hero, Ken Rosewall and Jimmy Connors, which Connors won 6-1, 6-1, 6-4, to my new mates' dismay.

I woke to a new day in a new city in a new country on my birthday, July 6, with a monster hangover and six dollars in my pocket. I had forgotten about banks being closed on the weekends. Luckily, I had prepaid my hotel, but the rest of my money was shut in the bank until Monday.

Coming from such a close community in Cork, knowing almost everyone, I was devastated walking the streets of Melbourne. No one—not one person—saluted me or said hello. I couldn't walk anywhere in Ireland for more than a minute without someone stopping me for a chat, or at least bidding me the time of day. The isolation scared me, it was worse to me than jail. At least in jail there would be some communication, but on the streets of Melbourne there was no oasis of friendship for me, not even a smile. Everyone was preoccupied with their own affairs. No one seemed to want to see the lost look in my eyes.

After two days of walking the streets, trying to familiarise myself with my new home town, I knew I was going to find it very hard to adjust to my new life. Mainly, the isolation and not knowing what was happening to Niall and Liz were the worst aspects. I was finding it difficult to sleep, still suffering from jetlag, and constantly thinking of the children. I would wake up, jump out of bed, thinking it was all a nightmare and that I was back in Ireland. I had no idea that this disturbed sleep pattern and nightmares would continue nightly for several years to come.

Monday didn't come soon enough for me—at least I could have a decent meal again and a few dollars in my pocket. But after that, what else was I to do? I thought I'd better get a newspaper and look up the jobs and flats-to-rent section. I was called by the hotel receptionist as I picked up my room key, 'There was a call for you, Mr Bowen.'

Oh, shit, the police must know I'm here, I thought. Who else would want me?

'A Mr Dallas. He left a number.'

I sighed with relief. My first communication in three days. Life was looking up. I left it till six to return his call.

'Hi, I'm returning Bob's call, it's Mike Bowen.'

'G'day, mate. Bob here. What are you doing?'

'I guess I'm lost, Bob. I don't know.'

'Listen mate, that hotel must be costing you a bomb. Why don't you come and crash with us until you get a job and a place to stay for yourself? I'll pick you up in about 45 minutes, OK?'

I put the phone down and cried. Someone cared, oh my God. Life sometimes throws us strange things. When we think all is lost, up comes a ray of sunshine.

Bob smiled. 'G'day, mate.'

'Bob, it's almost 7 pm and it's raining but you're dead right, it's a good day.'

'Twenty-three Walker Road, Clifton Hill, that's where we live, but we're going to meet Nigel at The Homebush for a countermeal and a few drinks first. Happy with that?'

I was just happy to have someone to talk to.

'Oh, by the way, we don't have an extra bed so you can share mine or use the fold-down couch.'

'I'll use the couch.'

'Oh, and I better let you know I really do prefer the company of guys, actually, to be honest I'm bisexual.'

'Thanks for telling me. I'll try not to tempt you too much.'

'Pity,' he replied. 'And you're such a nice guy. Not to worry, I'm sure we'll be good mates.'

'Bob, does this change the arrangements?'

'Shit no, mate. Don't you worry, none of us wanted you wasting your money on hotel bills, not with your limited funds.'

'Thanks for your honesty and generosity,' I found myself saying.

'Just buy Nigel a cask of claret every week. He owns the house. That'll keep him happy.'

Bob spent the next four weeks showing me around Melbourne in his taxi, at no cost of course. He introduced me to greyhound racing at Olympic Park and Sandown Park where I had many wins on Zulu Moss and Tamlie, two fabulous dogs who made me lots of money in the months to come.

I was star-struck when Bob introduced me to the MCG and Aussie Rules—such a sensational stadium. In my mind's eye I could see Ronnie Dalany run every step of that famous gold medal mile at the Olympics in 1956. I wondered if he had noticed the unique smell that I had noticed. What a strange thought to have. I looked around and savoured the moment. This was the reason I chose Melbourne to be my home for the next twelve years. What would happen if Ronnie had come second? Would I still have chosen Melbourne? God only knows. Life can be strange at times.

In the following weeks, Bob was proud to take me to see Essendon play at home at Windy Hill, Geelong at Geelong, North Melbourne at Arden Street, Hawthorn at Glenferrie Oval and Fitzroy at the Junction Oval. I loved the atmosphere and excitement and, of course, all the

Irish named players. One confused me though—Cowboy Neil. I thought, *Something's wrong here, no cowboys in Ireland.*

In spite of all the hoo-hah and the massive crowds at the games, when you grow up supporting another code of sport it's very difficult to change horses, so to speak. I came to the conclusion that it must be aerial ballet. The players seemed to all want to jump up on one another's backs and, in turning to handball, they appeared to want to do pirouettes. And I couldn't fathom the umpires. They seemed to have come from another planet—a species unto themselves. Shit, they would confuse anyone. It sure didn't help a dyslexic, confused Irishman. Take him to a footy game after four pints and he'll really think he's pissed.

Now, the goal umpires are another story in their Mr Sheen white coats, or are their coats borrowed from the asylum? To anyone who is non-Australian there is nothing more ridiculous in this world than watching the antics of a goal umpire signalling a goal. I'm sure brain surgeons didn't have to do as much training at uni to perfect their skills as the poor goal umpires, God help them.

... I had a vision of Mr Goal Umpire jumping out of bed on the morning of a match day in his white underpants and t-shirt with two flags under his arm looking at his wife and waving his flags, signalling a score, then sliding his wardrobe door open to reveal a full row of white coats and hats. He clutches his chin as he ponders which to wear for today's match. Plucking one from the middle after five minutes of contemplation, he hurries downstairs in the same stilted movements as he displays after a goal or point has been scored, waving his flags around frantically in the kitchen indicating breakfast is required. All in the midst of his two offspring, also dressed in white umpire regalia.

Upon finishing his breakfast, Mr Umpire stands to attention. Then moving back from the table, he signals a score to Mrs Umpire and their two siblings. On stepping out his front door, there is his pride and joy waiting to take him to the game: a 1964 Mini Minor. He pauses for a minute to suck in the fresh morning air, then every footy fan's nightmare—all the other doors in the street open and, guess what? In every doorway stands a man in full white regalia. Yes, it's Umpire Street. This is where they all live, locked away in a community unto themselves and a street full of Mini Minors. There can be no other explanation, at least from an Irishman's point of view, anyway . . .

I knew people in Ireland who were laughed at for a lot less. As a politician would say, 'In saying all that, let me say this': in spite of the wonderful atmosphere, huge crowds and magnificent stadiums, I honestly had no intention of becoming a regular footy fan. Ballet, yes, tiddly-winks, yes, watching grass grow, yes, footy—no, definitely no.

Bob also took responsibility for introducing me to all-night dinner sessions of Aussie wine and the good old Aussie barbecue. My first experience of the barbecue was when I was invited to bring a plate. So as not to cause my host any embarrassment, I thought I would bring a half dozen. When I arrived clutching my precious crockery, Bob slapped me on the back of the head, 'You silly Irish bastard, you're supposed to bring food.'

'They asked me to bring a plate Bob, you silly Aussie bastard.'

'What they meant was to bring food. Steak, sausages, chops and so on—get it?'

'Then why the fuck didn't they say so?'

'That's what "a plate" means.'

'Bob, a fucking plate is a plate and a fucking chop is a chop and you guys think us Irish are stupid, well the next time they invite me they better tell me what they want then I won't have to carry the dinner set and cutlery around with me, OK?'

Growing up in a culture of music and dance, I found it very strange that no one in my new home sang or danced after a few drinks. Strange and so sad because it's a wonderful way to express your joy and happiness. I put it down to the fact that they were all descendents of convicts and didn't have much to feel happy about.

CHAPTER NINE

A FOOTHOLD

NIGEL WAS GROWING restless by now with me a month sleeping on his couch and no job or signs of me moving into a place of my own, so it was obvious I had to do something. John Wilkinson, who was studying to be a lawyer, had a girlfriend named Judy who was looking for someone to share her unit in Springvale. Eighteen dollars a week plus gas, lights and phone bills so I jumped at it and moved the same day to Nigel's delight. I also got myself an interview for a job at what I thought was a light globe company called Mazda.

When I arrived at 9 am on Monday in High Street, Preston, I discovered it was Hershirl Motors, a Mazda motor car dealership.

Oh shit, well here goes.

'Hi. I'm looking for Ray Collins,' I asked at reception. A smiling bespeckled Ray Collins walked down the showroom, shook my hand firmly and warmly.

'G'day, Mike, let's get you in to see Herman. Herman is the MD and owner. I'm the sales manager.'

We entered Herman's glass surrounded office. He reached over his desk and shook my hand.

'Take a seat.' He was in his late forties, balding with a pleasant personality. The interview was direct and short.

'Do you know anything about Mazdas?'

'No.'

'Have you ever sold cars?'

'No.'

'How long have you lived in Australia?'

'Four-and-a-half weeks.'

'Where do you live?'

'Springvale.'

'Too far away,' he replied. End of interview. 'Sorry we can't help you.' Ray walked me to the door, shook my hand and thanked me for coming.

I stood on the pavement, looked up at the sign 'Hershirl Motors' and felt my blood boil. I stormed back into Herman's office.

'Listen here, Mister, until five minutes ago I thought a Mazda was a light globe. You advertised looking for a salesman, that's what I am and a bloody good one too, and what has the fact that I live in Springvale got to do with my ability to sell? I came thirteen thousand miles for this job, what's a few more to Springvale? I tell you what, I'll work here for nothing for a week and if I sell nothing it costs you nothing, but if I were you I wouldn't bet on that, because I didn't come thirteen thousand miles to starve.'

Ray entered with a surprised look on his face.

'Mike's joining us, Ray, for what I would imagine is going to be a long time. Would you organise a desk and anything he needs?' Herman shook my hand.

Ray walked me to my new desk in my new job saying, 'I have to say that was good, real good. You are one hell of a determined kid. Welcome to the car trade.' He shook his head, laughing. 'Light globe . . .' he muttered.

I now had my own home (shared though may it be), which gave me independence, a job and a car. Life was on a positive move. But nothing could give me comfort from the lonely nights and the homesickness was just about all I could bear. I missed the chit-chat of my friends and I missed my best mate and consoler, Stef. I missed the comforting smile of my dad and I missed being called, 'son'. I was devastated by the loss of Niall and Liz. Still, my Aunt Mary's words continued to ring in my ears so I made a slight alteration: 'I may feel I am in the shit on this side of the world, but I don't have to live in it. Now go out and there and make a name for yourself. You're a very bright young man.'

God, how I took comfort in her encouraging words. They were my saviour on so many days and nights when the lonesomeness was too much to bear and I thought of ending it all. This is the pattern of thoughts for one who is isolated, and it takes a will of steel to fight it. Not receiving a reply to my weekly letters I was now writing to Serica's mother only ever asking for forgiveness didn't help either.

I took comfort in my new job working seven days a week. As I didn't have much else to do, I figured I might as well make money. I soon became as comfortable as a duck in water and in no time I was receiving awards and bonuses for my efforts.

The Aussies continued to put us Irish down, calling us mad Irish or Paddy, and then there was the continuous barrage of questions. What do you think of the troubles in Ireland? Are you Catholic or Protestant? How many leprechauns do you have in your family? Do you have telly in Ireland? To which I usually replied, 'Oh yes, but it's only gas and they're having it converted to electricity next year. Sometimes they came back at me with, 'How do gas tellies work?' Now who's stupid!

I wisely concealed my frustration and anger. After all, I was in Australia to make a life and money, not enemies. I had to learn to dodge and weave and reply smartly and make them think. So my answers were quite challenging. For instance, 'Are you Irish?' to which I would reply, 'Yes, but only by accident, I am Australian by choice. What about yourself, by accident or choice?' Usually a glum-faced reply. Or again when asked, 'Is that an Irish accent?' My usual reply, 'Gee, you're perceptive,' or, 'I'm not sure. I'm minding it for one of my neighbours who's gone on holidays for a few weeks.'

In spite of all the negative comments, I continued to strive in my job and make new acquaintances. That is, except for female comfort because I must have smelt like rotten fish. It took a bit of getting used to having a shower every day. You'd be lucky if you had a wash once a week or once a month in Ireland. I can tell you, there's no need for one in Ireland as no one gets themselves into a sweat—maybe into the shit, but not a sweat.

I wrote to Clifford in Ireland to inform him of my whereabouts as I took him as a trusted friend, later to discover otherwise. He wrote back to me asking me to send him his fare saying he would join me. It was November 1974 and Australia was about to change its immigration policy so that no more aliens would be allowed in without qualifying. I sent Clifford his fare hoping he would join me before the new rules came in and thought maybe his company would help me adjust more to my new home. After all, he told me he had been comforting my mum and dad in my absence and that gave me some sort of peace within myself.

I stood there at Tullamarine airport just days before the November deadline waiting for Clifford's plane to arrive, hopefully bringing me photos and news of home and the children. My overwhelming joy in seeing him soon turned to sadness as he told me Serica was now being screwed by every Tom, Dick and Harry. My mum and dad had virtually disowned me and Mary was having an affair with an old school friend of mine (not that that was any of my business).

He seemed to take delight in being the bearer of bad news and watching my sadness grow. He continued to rub salt into my wounds at every opportunity which was not the medicine I needed now. I was hoping for some good news but not one word of comfort came from his lips. He emphasised that, due to the statute of limitations, I could not return to Ireland, if ever, and it sent chills down my spine and my heart sank in my chest. How could I never see Ireland again or Niall and Liz?

Please, God, don't let it be.

The day was a barrage of questions looking for some reassurance in Clifford's answers with little comfort. We talked and drank our way through the day and night with no thought of time or going to bed. I didn't want to be sober with the pain.

On the home front, I was fed up kipping in sleeping bays and on camping beds which is all I had to sleep on. The thought of sleeping on a real bed after four months was real exciting and a wonderful reacquaintance with a real bed was about to happen that day and not an hour too soon.

I had organised to take over Ray Collins's third floor flat in Bendigo Street, Elwood, overlooking the beach—a real bachelor's delight. Everything was pre-paid rental with the exception of the TV. Unfortunately I was ripped off; paying $350 to my new manager at work for a black and white 19-inch. Still, I felt proud that I paid for everything, even Clifford's airfare, and that I had a good job at which I was successful. It all helped ease the pain, guilt and loneliness.

No sooner had I moved to Elwood, than the smell of fish must have left me for it was like I had a new identity. Women seemed to come from everywhere, from dropping in on Sundays for a cup of coffee or tea and a lie out on the balcony to inviting me to dinner and barbecues. What was so different now? I couldn't pull a trick last month. Now it was like the heavens opened. Maybe my Irish accent sounded cute in summer, I have no idea. I wasn't complaining, yet underneath I was still homesick and hurting but, as the Aussies say, 'rooting takes the pain away.' This was true to some extent, but was not nearly as gruesome as going through another period of 'all women are game' as a get-back payment. If you've been hurt then you hurt someone else—it's the adults game we rarely admit to.

I still wrote my regular Friday letter to Serica's mum and never a reply.

Clifford worked as a watch salesman and moved in with me to share the flat but contributed zero to the household expenses. However, it didn't bother me as I could afford the upkeep of our snazzy Elwood bachelor pad. From the first day I started work I sent monies to my mother for the children for school and whatever they needed. I wouldn't send it to Mary. Firstly, I wanted her to claim her full entitlement as a single deserted mother and also if I sent the money to her she might lie and say I never really sent any and so I sent the monies to my mother. At least she would know I was doing the right thing. I may have left my children but I never failed to support them—never. No one was going to accuse me of lacking in my responsibilities if I cocked up. I wasn't going to fuck up. If they were going to be short, it wasn't going to be my fault.

I understood about responsibility, I learned it from my sister when Liza was in hospital for those long periods and my father didn't come home for days and weeks due to his drinking problems. She was my mother, she took the load in Liza's absence and only when the job got too much for her and she came down with rheumatic fever did my Aunt Mary take on my care. So I know how essential it is to have a responsible carer and also to be responsible for others. Human beings are precious cargo and children more so.

I thought by helping Clifford come to Australia and get set up here it would ease my lonesomeness for home and all those I loved there but instead, he became a huge burden. Firstly, I hadn't realised he had a dual personality: on one side pleasant (but never sweet) and then the real rotten dark side after a few drinks. Everyone was his enemy and, when he couldn't find any enemies, he vented his anger on me. It used to take all of my attention to try and keep him out of trouble and humour him. Bob and nearly all of my new friends shunned me as they didn't want to be on the receiving end of Clifford's constant jibes.

I sometimes thought he was envious of my strengths and my interactions with other people, and because he was not 'top dog' on this patch, he took on the spoilt child syndrome, but more vindictive, much more. He never showed appreciation for anything, not for the airfare I sent him or the fact that he was living rent free and eating free. It was only aggro and when there was a shortage he would create some more. He would insult and ridicule me and then phone Liza and tease her in relation to my whereabouts, which was devastating to a mother who was already in pain not knowing where her son was nor hearing from him. He seemed to delight in inflicting pain into people's hearts. Growing up, I had seen lots of nasty things on the streets of Cork and had met some awful characters, but Clifford brought a new dimension to cruelty.

Christmas seemed to come upon us quickly and I was amazed when Ron Tucker, my new sales manager, invited Clifford and me to Christmas dinner in his home in Dingley. Firstly, I was amazed he invited Clifford considering he knew Clifford's form and secondly, I didn't particularly get on very well with him, although he did say on many occasions I was the best salesman he had worked with. Considering it was my first Christmas in Australia and no one else would invite us anywhere anyway—and why would they unless they wanted to start World War III with Clifford at the helm?—I was most grateful for the invitation and saw it as a privilege. Unlike my counterpart.

I was fascinated with the idea of having hot turkey in the high temperatures by the pool which was a total contrast to Ireland. Such a very odd experience for me having never known anything but a freezing cold, wintry Christmas in Gurranbraher. *I wonder what Ronnie Dalany is doing now, I'll bet he doesn't have shorts on like me today. And Serica: has she given a thought for me?* I wondered if the gossipers had given up on us—I supposed not. Probably not for years. After all, the Irish love to carry a good story for a long time. *And what of Niall and Liz? Will they ever understand? Will their hearts grow bitter with the passing of time and from the mutilated, twisted versions of the whole affair of Liza's son? Or will the old Irish saying 'Time is a wonderful healer' come true for me and everyone else?* Only time would tell.

Liza and Mick must have been devastated with the absence of their only son and, no doubt, Breda was equally devastated missing her only brother. I knew Aunt Mary was missing me but I also knew she was praying desperately hard for me to succeed.

Stef and Tom Ellis would miss me for our regular Christmas Eve drinks and jam sessions in the local in Glanmire. This was the first time I'd not been there in almost a decade. Stef, Tom, Tom's brother George, and his friend, Frank, and myself would always go to the pub in the afternoon and stay to all hours every Christmas Eve, for a jam session and a sing-song. What a magic way to remember Christmas.

Tom, George and Frank were also Protestants and were wonderful friends. We used to have great music sessions at Tom's beautiful home in Glanmire. When I say they were Protestants, I mean it in the most respectful way, for it was not common in the 1960s for Proddies and Micks to socialise in Cork. We did regardless.

My thoughts were interrupted by the heated discussion going on between Clifford and Ron, so I quickly intervened. I thanked the Tuckers for their generosity and apologised profusely for having to leave on short notice due to a violent migraine—any excuse to avoid another brawl and embarrassment. Clifford vented his anger by pushing me into the pool knowing I was a non-swimmer. I retrieved my pride by laughing it off. So much for my first Christmas in Australia.

Clifford was never the companion I needed so desperately to put sanity back into my life. At times I felt I was the only person in the universe. No one seemed to care or understand the isolation I felt and I suppose why should they? After all, it was my dilemma in my world. I desperately needed a soulmate and Clifford was driving the few friends I had away. At times the isolation and the nightmares were so bad . . . why not just end it all?

But always in my desperate hours two things came into my mind. Firstly, the time I stepped in between Mick and Liza while he was in one of his drunken rages. It was the one and only time in my life Mick hit me and I ran from the house in St. Anthony's Road into the freezing, rain-soaked night wandering the streets of Cork looking for a saint to come and rescue me and keep me warm and safe in heaven. I wanted to never again feel hurt, cold, wet and hungry—an awful dilemma for an eight-year-old. I consoled myself with the thought that if I were to die then it should have been when God had the perfect opportunity, when I had my lung operation, so if He didn't take me then, He must have wanted me to stay for a good reason, and that hadn't arrived yet. The second thing that came to my mind was my Aunt Mary's undying belief in me and my ultimate success in life. She really believed I was special.

The letters still flowed weekly to Serica's mum and never a reply. I thought she might at least see my persistent apologies as a gesture of my honest love for Serica and a sincere attempt to heal what damage I had done, but no such forgiveness was forthcoming. If her reason for not replying was to hurt me the most, then it was working to the maximum, but I didn't hold that against her.

I spent every spare minute I had at work between the New Year and March trying to avoid Clifford and his uncontrollable aggro. He was worse than a drunken father for at least a drunken father is generally only aggro when drunk whereas Clifford was that way all the time. He even extended his aggression to racism when he told a beautiful Sri Lankan girl I was dating called Dian, 'You're black, I hate blacks. If I wanted blacks in my life I would have gone to South Africa where I could have had a dozen of them working for me for ten dollars a week.' Clifford never made a remark like that to a guy, he knew how to pick his mark. To Dian's credit she gave the comment the same treatment that a good Sri Lankan batsman would give an Australian fast bowler: to just push it to one side. This annoyed him no end. Of course, like the others, Dian soon moved on to less insulting friends.

CHAPTER TEN

WINTER TURNS TO SPRING

CLIFFORD DID PERSUADE me to go for a night out to celebrate the Moomba Festival (the largest community festival in Australia) and St. Patrick's week. It was the first Friday of Moomba, 1975, and I hadn't seen him for quite some time. I felt maybe he had come to his senses. We did a pub crawl of Elizabeth Street and listened to the stage acts that were playing in the open air there and we finally ended up at the Celtic Club. I noticed two girls at a table and asked if we could join them, to which came the polite reply, 'No.' And like a good little doggie who is reprimanded for soiling the carpet, I skulked away to the next table with my tail between my legs. Clifford soon joined me.

'Fuck, what happened?' was his response to my knock-back.

'They wanted to be on their own,' I whispered through my clenched teeth. I should have known what Clifford's reaction was going to be. It came anyway.

'Fuck that, let me talk to them.'

'Don't don't don't,' I begged. 'We're here for a drink. Remember what you said? It was going to be just a celebration night, not an aggro one.' He seemed to heed my response but insisted on speaking Gaelic and was far from complimentary about the girls.

Clifford's continuing comments about the girls provoked one of them to say, 'Would you please ask your vulgar-mouthed friend to kindly tone down?' Then she gave him an apple to keep his mouth shut. Clifford hadn't realised the girls also spoke fluent Gaelic for they had obviously understood every word.

I apologised profusely, to Clifford's annoyance. He picked up the apple, hit me on the head with it and stormed out of the club leaving me and the two girls in disbelief. I should have known better.

God must have been very close by me then, because I have no other explanation for the way I got out of the stupid situation I now found myself in. I mustered up the courage to offer to buy the girls a forgive-me-for-my-friend's-stupid-carry-on drink. To my surprise, they were most understanding and asked me to join them. I was overwhelmed considering Clifford's rude comments towards them. They introduced themselves as Sophie and Helen. They were sisters from Galway. We spent the rest of the night reminiscing about all the familiar places we knew in Galway and Helen told me of her time in New York. Helen and I hit it off straight away for we had frequented the same pubs in Galway and New York, where I had worked occasionally a few years ago.

I was in seventh heaven talking to the girls until I heard the old familiar call, 'Time Gentlemen Please. Come on now, drink up.' I didn't want the conversation to end. Without even thinking I said, 'Can I take you home, Helen?' to which both girls looked at me bewildered, as the words that came out of my mouth didn't sound the way I'd intended. God must surely have been watching over me for Helen replied, 'Only if you behave yourself, because if you don't, I have another apple here and I'll hit you with it,' to which we all laughed.

Helen's apartment was in the Hacienda Block on Acland Street, about a mile or so from mine. It was a tidy, one-bedroom on the second floor. Her manner was gracious, elegant, and most pleasant. After the formalities of coffee and kisses, we agreed to meet for dinner the following night. And I can tell you I couldn't wait for it to come soon enough.

As always, I was punctual, and rather than go out for dinner, Helen cooked Nasi Goreng and we talked into the early hours. No 'Time, Gentlemen' this time; just easy, flowing conversation.

Helen pointed out the time when it was 2.30 am and indicated she did not expect me to spend the night to which I cordially complied. Nonetheless, I was as happy as a pig in shit, I felt I had found a soul-mate. Again, we agreed to meet for lunch the next day, Sunday. I felt maybe my life was about to take a turn for the better, so again I could hardly wait. I had heard so many times tomorrow never comes, but as sure as hell it was coming this time.

❀   ❀   ❀

I woke to a beautiful sunny Australian morning as if the angels were turning it on for me. I needed something good in my life and I felt special again. I was caught in a triangle of confusion. I was still guilty for feeling good when I missed the children so much and still didn't feel in any way comfortable about the whole Serica affair. But there was a strange feeling of tranquillity about being 13,000 miles from home. As least there were no gossipers and no Bishop Casey to give me the third degree about sex and guilt.

After a jog around Albert Park Lake and a refreshing cup of coffee, I got dressed to impress and, just in case we got delayed with our afternoon discovering Melbourne together, I brought a change of clothes. Helen was concerned about this as she thought I was expecting to stay overnight. I explained I intended to take her dancing at The

Powerhouse in Albert Park with Marcia Hines and the Daley Wilson Big Band and therefore needed a suit to look gentlemanly and reasonably formal. And I wanted to impress her by taking her to dinner first. She responded with a huge enthusiastic kiss and hug. This told me without words the misunderstanding was forgiven.

We sat around for a couple of hours in the 1960s hippy style of crossed legs, solving the woes of the world. I soaked up every minute of the joy of pleasant conversation. With every word from Helen's lips I was becoming more enchanted with her gracious femininity—she sure was a classy lady. An excellent dinner and dancing was all that was required to cap off a perfect day, or so I thought until I was invited to stay over.

When I woke up on Monday morning I decided I was about to take a major step in a different direction. I wasn't prepared to have Clifford interfere in my life anymore, so I picked up my clothing from Bendigo Street and moved in with Helen. The month that followed was just pure bliss. No intruders in my life, no Clifford to pamper, no Mary and wet beds, no Tralee gossipers. But the nightmares of Niall and Liz continued and every time I heard a Jimmy Webb, Charlie Rich, Tom Jones or a Dawn song, instantly Tralee and all the associated pain rushed back. This was another issue I had to deal with and could not let it break me.

A new world of music was opening up to me, a world now made up of Johnny Farnham, Sherbet, Marcia Hines, Doug Ashdown, Ross Ryan, The Ted Mulry Gang, Jon English and John Paul Young. This was a completely different type of music to the kind I had grown up with: Jim Reeves, Hank Locklin, and all the great songwriters such as Gordon Lightfoot, Don McLean, Simon and Garfunkle, Jim Webb, Neil Diamond and Roy Orbison. I missed the heart-wrenching lyrics of those guys but I was optimistic that the Aussie counterparts would leave their imprint too. Time would help me embrace the new music. I made a decision to start to write my own songs, mainly reflections of my own life and the old loves and torments of my experiences.

I was beginning to like poetry and took to it like a duck to water. My first poem was, 'So You Want to Be Part of Me, You Want My Name.' In my new environment I felt I could try all those things that I always wanted to do without fear of comments like, 'Who does he think he is? His old man was a docker and they never had nothin', not a penny to their name and, for chrisakes, isn't that just Liza's son, is he a wanker, or what? Who the fuck does he think he is?'

I just loved the freedom to be who I really was and the thought of being able to achieve what I wanted to achieve excited me no end. I knew when I let go of the apron strings of mother Ireland then Aunt Mary's belief in me would be fulfilled. Sure, life would continue to throw up its fair share of challenges—and I expected nothing less—except now I felt I was better equipped to cope. I promised myself I would have my music recorded and my poetry published one day. I would show them all.

Yes, I may have been born into shit conditions, but I would be strong enough to use my background as a stepping-stone towards my future, not an invisible barrier. I would write about all the things that surrounded my life in music and poetry. Yes, I would show them that you didn't have to be born with a silver spoon in your mouth to be good or smart and I would show those people at the New School in Gurranabraher what a talent they missed out on when they wouldn't let me join the school band. And the fact that I was dyslexic, and not a fool, wouldn't prevent me from achieving my goal. *Gurranabraher, I promise to make you proud of me*. I could visualise my Aunt Mary reading *The Cork Echo* or *The Cork Examiner* (or *The Irish Examiner*, as it's now become known since going national) to my nan, Liz. 'Sure, didn't I tell you, mother, he would turn out to be a wonderful person?' and Mary would smile from ear to ear and be so proud. In view of the circumstances under which I left Ireland, I felt I could not return as anything other than a success, and I felt comfortable and confident with my new mantle.

In view of my new relationship I reduced my apology letters to Serica's mother to fortnightly. It was nine months since my departure from Ireland and I had received no reply. My heart was so saddened with the lack of response I felt like a criminal. Surely she could have said she understood even if she didn't forgive me. I ceased believing time was a wonderful healer.

It was 17 May, 1975, and Tammy Wynette had a number one hit, 'Stand By Your Man' and I thought, *Oh my God, what a joke!* This surely was not meant to include me, at least not in my life up to the present day, but hopefully that would change too.

After a month with Helen, life was wonderful and she was a beautiful, loving and caring person and a sheer delight to be with. Her world revolved around making my life as comfortable and happy as possible. We agreed to make our relationship permanent, so we decided to look for a bigger and more comfortable place for ourselves. We called in at Bendigo Street to pick up the remainder of my clothes and, to my amazement, the flat was empty except for my TV sitting in the corner. Everything else was gone—not even the toilet paper was left.

Clifford had gone and disposed of everything and left a whopper of a telephone bill behind for me to pay. I didn't care, in fact, I was relieved. It didn't matter about the cost, it was worth it to have him out of my life and there was certainly no reason for Helen to have to put up with his tantrums.

Our new flat in Toorak Road, South Yarra, was a romantic's dream, as was my relationship. The months rolled on, but the nightmares of the children continued and the fortnightly letters to Serica's mum continued, always and only apologies.

One night while watching TV the doorbell rang. Clifford stood there. Somehow he had got hold of my new address. 'Mike, I think I killed someone. He was a poof and he tried it on me.' I had known Clifford too long by now and he was a sensationalist. He was also drunk as usual. I gave him a drink and told him to go home and I would sort everything out with the police in the morning. It was the first time I've ever known him to depart quietly and I was amazed to say the least. Needless to say, I didn't go to the police and, of course, I heard no further from Clifford—just another one of his antics.

Helen and I were so happy just being on our own with no outside interference and spent our weekends discovering Melbourne and Victoria in general. It was so exciting to throw off the shackles of conservative Ireland. I never wrote to, nor received any letters from Mum or Dad for fear of someone finding our exactly where I was in case I was arrested and deported. I usually converted the monies I sent to Mum for the children into Papua New Guinean or New Zealand currencies just to keep the hounds off the trail, so to speak. And I rarely walked on the same side of the street as a policeman for fear of being recognised. So while life was bliss, it wasn't without it's fair share of concerns.

Herman sold Hershirl Motors and I was flattered to receive a phone call from David Syers, the sales manager for Mazda, inviting me to join Mazda Motors' head office in La Trobe Street. Obviously my reputation in sales was growing. The new job fitted me like a glove. They were fabulous people to work with; such dignity and class is the only way to describe that firm of professionals. David Syers was the consummate manager, with enormous people skills and a fabulous personality. I felt he was the one I could learn most from in my future sales career.

I couldn't imagine life getting any better, well, guess what? It did! Helen and I decided to buy a house together in Mornington, a bayside suburb about 50 kilometres from Melbourne. The first thing that came to mind was, *I can't believe it; the kid from Gurranabraher can afford to buy a house; the same kid whose family could only afford soup for dinner on Sundays can actually afford to buy a house.* It was an overwhelming feeling. Australia was giving me every opportunity to pick myself up and was helping me to get some sort of normality into my life—well, as normal as I thought it could be. But I knew in my heart of hearts that I would push the boundaries for I felt that the sky was the limit and, therefore, I would take whatever opportunities came along to further myself.

I started to chase some of the publishing companies regarding recording and publishing my songs. I was feeling rather cocky, but the music industry has a very blunt way of taking the wind out of your sails. But that wasn't going to deter me with my ambitions to be in some way recognised and influential in the musical industry.

The springtime of my life had just tapped me on the shoulder and I was enjoying a quality of living that I had only ever dreamt about. I had a job I liked and at which I was successful, the power to make choices in my life I'd never known before and to live the life I always wanted but, more importantly, there were no gossipers on this side of the world to gnaw away at my happiness. Helen and I grew closer with every passing day and we both grew in confidence. It was perfect timing that we met when we both needed someone to enhance our lives and we equally contributed to making the most of it. I loved the role of de facto husband, and couldn't wait to make our relationship official. So I set about the formalities of annulment or divorce from Mary.

Sophie, Helen's sister, recommended that I go to see a priest she knew who would give me some guidance on the matter. I was petri-fied of what he might say regarding my past life and commitments to the children. I had no idea of the road that this journey might take me on. (Speaking of divorce, I hadn't known anyone who was divorced, let alone how to go about it.)

Father Merriott was the most understanding and compassionate clergy person I had ever met. He gave me back my dignity in abun-dance during the two hours I spent with him.

'Your life is yours, son, and we all make mistakes. I am not immune just because I am a priest. You can only give it your best shot and that's all, and we don't always get it right. God never said if you fail you are doomed. All He ever said was if you fail, let me help you get it right next time. You have your whole life ahead of yourself, and make it a better one this time. But whatever you do, don't forget your commitment to your children regardless of now or the future. Just like God is your father, you will always be theirs, no matter what. If you love this woman and she loves you, go off and organise a divorce and marry her before you get any older. Don't waste your time and money on an annulment, it's only a revenue job for the Church.'

He embraced me and wished me good luck. God certainly wrote the script for that meeting with Father Merriott. Though it was raining all day, I couldn't help feeling special. It was better than winning any lottery—who said money was everything? So I set about putting the mechanism of divorce in place and I was anxious to be part of it, so I organised to have the papers drafted up myself because I wanted it to be an honest statement and not driven by the legal fraternity.

The papers were drafted up in accordance and I sent them to a solicitor in Cork to be served to Mary and a date was set for the hearing in six weeks time. The next month was consumed with worry as to how it would be received in Ireland, and also what reaction the children might have regardless of their age. The month dragged by, and finally a response, which dumbfounded me:

'Dear Mr Bowen

We do not wish to act on your behalf as we feel you left your wife and children in a despicable and disgraceful manner. Therefore, we are returning your documents as we advised your wife not to respond to this ungodly act.'

On the day of the divorce hearing the judge asked me if I had organised to have the divorce papers served to Mary. 'Yes, Your Honour, and this was the reply.' I handed him the brown envelope. He carefully read the letter and responded, 'You've had enough problems with this lot in Ireland in your life. I'm not going to add to it. Divorce granted. And good luck, son, in your new life.'

And so a new chapter in my life began.

CHAPTER ELEVEN

WINDOWS TO MY SOUL

HELEN DECIDED TO visit Ireland with her sister for their parents' golden wedding anniversary. Some undoubtedly have the magic to last 50 years. It hit me that I wouldn't be able to go. Whatever confidence I had accumulated left me in an instant. I was devastated. I was petrified that Helen wouldn't come back from Ireland and I'd be alone and isolated once again. I was being totally irrational, but I couldn't see it then.

Of course she had to go, all her family were reuniting for the event. It was a once-in-a-lifetime occasion for Helen and it was silly of me to wallow in self-pity. I simply couldn't go and risk being arrested— not a very smart step forward—so I swallowed my pride and accepted the fact that I was exiled for twelve years and not a day less. Helen would spend five weeks in Ireland and I would baby-sit the new house, do the usual chores and be bombarded with Peter Allen's rendition of 'Rio' which was a big hit at the time.

The five weeks dragged; every day felt like a year. I missed my soulmate something awful. On her return we decided to marry and we set a date. I wrote to Mum and Dad to tell them of the pending wedding arrangements. Their response was to come for the occasion so Helen and I quickly changed the date and brought it forward to ensure they wouldn't be able to attend. Helen and I weren't quite ready for a visit from my parents, especially my mother, though there were no problems with Dad.

One Saturday night, Helen and I attended an Irish dance at the Chelsea Town Hall. Looking over my glass of Victoria Bitter beer I noticed a blonde girl with a rather slim guy over on the other side of the room. I nudged Helen, 'I think I know that blonde over there.'

'Oh yeah, is there a blonde you don't know?'

'Honestly, I think she's from Cork. I'll just go over and ask. Back in a minute.' What were the odds of Eireen Shine—a girl I worked with in Rudman's Paint Factory in Blarney Street, Cork—being there? The proverbial million-to-one, I guess.

I had worked at Rudman's learning the skills of paint making and tinting with a very humorous pair of practical-joking lads called Humphrey Sullivan and Jim Dunlea. Never a dull moment—best described as a kindergarten for adults! If we spent as much time working as we did practical-joking, I'm sure our skills would have been priceless.

Jim bought an old banger of a car which he kept spotless. Mind you, it didn't go very well, but who cared? It looked good. On one occasion, Humphrey and I decided it needed a change of image. So while Jim was out one day doing deliveries for the company, Humphrey and yours truly hand-painted Jim's black pride and joy green. Not just any old green mind you: British racing green. And to make matters worse, we wallpapered the inside for good measure.

Words could not describe Jim's disbelief on his return. A week of silence was our punishment before life returned to normal, or should I say abnormal. Some weeks later, on Jim's return from another errand, his newly glossed green car was black again, up on blocks, minus wheels, seats and steering wheel. Our sentence was another week of silence from Jim and so continued the practical jokes.

I can only say how much I admired the patience of our foreman manager, Donald Ford, a more kind and understanding boss you couldn't wish for. How he never lost his patience with us child-hearted adults I'll never know. Donald is the same guy who did a tireless job for soccer in Munster for many years.

'Well, excuse me, can I kindly have a passionate kiss please?' I said to the blonde as her husband looked on gob-smacked.

'Jesus Christ, Michael Bowen! What are you doing here?' she said with amazement.

'I'm waiting for a kiss.'

John Shine jumped up first; not quite what I was expecting, but better than a slap in the mouth. The three of us must have looked like loonies as we kissed and danced up and down for what seemed like ages. Helen was quite bemused by all our shenanigans; we were like school kids who had been lost and found again.

Over the next month, we caught up every day to natter and reminisce. So delighted were we with the friendship, I asked John to be best man at our wedding for he was now my best mate. I began to buy discount beer in the city for him every Friday and deliver it to him on my way home. More often than not we would drink it together. John was such a funny guy, a brick-cleaner by trade, while Eireen worked part-time and looked after their two young daughters.

After polishing off John's discount Friday special, it would not be unusual for him to run down to the pub for an extra few. God forbid if the drink-driving laws were in force then for John and I would have been locked up forever. But I must admit, I can't remember being as drunk after a gutful of booze in those days as I would be after a fraction of booze these days.

Kenlock in the Dandenong Ranges was the place of our wedding. It was a really lovely day. The bride (looking gorgeous), and John and I in blue velvet suits. John, being typical John, told me he that he couldn't see the value in buying a new pair of black shoes just for one day so he rented a pair just for the wedding. Thirteen in all was the full list of attendees. So good was our sing-song that two other wedding parties joined us to boost our numbers dramatically and we proceeded to lift the roof off Kenlock. Oh, what a night it was!

The next morning, the bride and groom left for the Gold Coast in southern Queensland for two weeks to recover, and John duly returned his rented pair of shoes and received his $60 deposit back.

We prepared ourselves for Mum and Dad's visit on our return. Julie Covington was still singing the *Evita* classic 'Don't Cry for Me, Argentina' after a lengthy stay in the charts.

In spite of time moving on, the letters continued to Serica's mum, though less regularly than before, apologising and begging for forgiveness. I often wondered what might have been had I continued living in Ireland. I still missed the constant salutes of the passers-by in Shandon Street, and the casual drop-in for a pint and a chat. I tried not to think about it too much because it broke my heart, but never a day went by that I didn't hear Aunt Mary's words driving me on to better things, 'Go on, son, make a name for yourself; don't just be known as Liza's son.'

We got the guest room prepared for the arrival of Mum and Dad, both scared of what their reaction might be. I so desperately wanted Mum to treat Helen with all the respect she deserved, and not as 'the other woman'. Yes, Mum was going to be a handful. I prayed a lot that she would be understanding. Dad would be easy about the whole thing, nothing like that would ever bother Dad. In those days, as long as life was easy, he wasn't bothered.

We so wanted to make them enjoy their visit, we were proud of what we had achieved: our gorgeous new house, we both had good jobs, and no debts. Surely Liza would see that I had turned my life around, and she would be proud of her son. The anticipation of their arrival was both scary and exciting. I was so looking forward to having intimate man-to-man conversations with Dad. I wanted to tell him everything, but I think most of all I wanted to tell him how beautiful it was to wake up in a dry bed in the morning and to not want to be away from my home and wife all the time. I wanted to tell him how good it was to never have to raise my voice in anger or frustration, how good it was to be able to have the opportunity to write and play guitar without having to go to my room and sing under my breath. I wanted to tell him how much I missed the children and I wanted him to know how it was breaking my heart. I wanted him to put his arms around me and hold me tight and tell me he loved me and was proud of me and all was forgiven.

In my heart I felt such miracles were limited, but I must've been one of the lucky ones because for the five weeks they spent with us over Christmas and New Year's, I got my miracle and more with my dad. I told him of every drink and every affair I ever had and he came clean to me about his alcoholic addiction and his turbulent relationship with Mum. He explained how as a docker on Cork's quays, the work was hard and the relationship with his mates was much the same as an extended family so when he worked and his mates didn't have work or money, he would take them drinking and they would do the same for him when he wasn't working. The work was very infrequent and that explained why Mum got very little money from him when he worked, because then it was his turn to shout his mates. So very little, if any, money was left for Liza. Mick told me later of many things he regretted and was ashamed of in his past—including his mistreatment of Breda as a child.

I latched onto every word he told me for I knew he was aching inside. We cried and laughed a lot and I found a father I never knew I had. I told him I understood. On the other hand, Liza was being typical Liza; forever making me feel guilty and encouraging me to return to Ireland. She was the typical scorned Irish mother, as demanding as a two-year-old, and cutting me down at every opportunity. She was patronisingly pleasant to Helen.

In spite of Liza's discontent, we did manage to show them around our lovely city of Melbourne and the state of Victoria, and we introduced them to many of our new friends. Still, I knew no matter what I did for Liza, she would not be happy.

My heart was saddened on the day they departed for Ireland. Dad and I hugged and cried for a long time. He told me he loved me and was enormously proud, and it broke my heart that Liza didn't. I cried for days afterwards, looking at the pictures of the children, Niall and Liz, and I missed my dad so much. Now I had another advocate to drive me on to success.

For the following months I reminisced on the stories that Liza and Mick had told Helen and I. It was just fabulous to get all the news. I was grateful to God for being good to me. But then as soon as good news comes, shit happens. We got an urgent call from John and Eireen one Sunday saying they were returning to Ireland as Eireen's dad was dying of cancer and they would not be returning to Australia. Helen and I spent the next week counselling and consoling both of them. They were going to sell up everything and leave in a month. The following Saturday night the phone rang on six occasions and each time before I got to answer it, it stopped. I was furious getting in and out of bed. However, the next morning the phone rang again at 8 am and the culprit was revealed. It was a very drunk John Shine on the other end.

'How's it going, old son? Where the fuck were you when I was ringing you all of last night?' he said joyously. 'And what night was last night and what happens on Saturday nights?'

To which I delighted in replying, 'Guys like you get hopelessly pissed and ring and annoy the fuck out of people like me, right?'

'Nope, wrong,' he stuttered. 'Guys like me win the lotto.'

'WHAT?' I screamed.

'Yep, won the lotto. And the party started straight away so whenever you're ready, drop in because it will be on all week. So get your arse over here because when the booze runs out, we're off home to Ireland.'

Some guys get lucky in Ireland and who says you can't get lucky in Australia? True to his word, the party lasted a week and John's good luck was our sad loss of our very, very good friends. I suppose it was inevitable that John and Eireen would return home one day as they never really settled in Australia. It took Helen a long time to get over losing our friends. We sadly missed them.

It wasn't long after that when Helen broke the news that she was expecting. We were overcome with joy and anticipation of the new arrival. We couldn't believe our good fortune. We didn't care if it was a boy or girl as long as he or she would be healthy, that was all that mattered.

There was some bad news on another front: Mazda was closing its retail section and I would have to move to another company. There was no shortage of offers, but still I was very sad as they had been a wonderful company to work for. I would surely miss my good mates. I will always be grateful to David Syers who showed me a whole new way to approach my work with dignity, style and confidence.

Danny Hewitt, who came from the Falls Road area of Belfast, was the used car manager at Dandenong Mazda and he persuaded me to join him in the new car department. I was fortunate in getting to work with some lovely people and unfortunate to work with one absolutely rotten individual, a nasty devious little person in Kevin Anderson who was general manager and who hated Danny Hewitt with a passion. Therefore, as I befriended Danny and as I am Irish, he did everything he could to make life miserable for me. When I started to be named top salesman on a regular basis it annoyed him even more (wherever he is today, I hope he found his peace). Thank God you only meet one or two of those people in a lifetime. Come to think of it, Clifford and Kevin would have made a formidable pair.

Danny was married to Sharon, also from Belfast, and they had two boys, Brian and Adrian; two lovely kids. We became close friends. The new manager was the wonderful, joyous Barry Mills and Danny's assistant was Greg Mead, a Vietnam vet who told me a lot about his experiences in the war. Ray Laird was the finance and insurance manager, who spent a lot of his spare time teaching and explaining about shares and the sharemarket to me. Joan Kavanagh was the office manager and her husband, Michael, was a wonderful and funny bloke who I became very close friends with, and was inspired to write about him through his illness with cancer.

Helen and I asked Danny to be godfather to our new arrival. On 1 September, 1979 at 4 am, Jonathan Joseph Bowen was born after a very difficult delivery which I attended. I can put my hand on my heart and swear that there is no way I would ever be a woman and go through a pregnancy and give birth. It's so, so hard on a woman—and I had the cheek to think I had it tough in my time. All I can say is, thank God I wasn't born female.

I was over the moon on his arrival. I had never seen such a good looking baby, he was just beautiful. I was so proud of him and his glowing mum. I was so excited I wanted to tell the whole world, so I bought a dozen bottles of champagne, a dozen bottles of moselle, two-dozen bottles of beer, a dozen chickens and two dozen bread rolls and took them to work with me to celebrate. It was a hilarious day. Everyone got as drunk as skunks. God knows how none of us got fired after such a display.

What a pity the people of Melbourne didn't flock to Dandenong to buy their new Mazdas on that September day, because none of us were in any condition to negotiate a sales deal and they surely would have got a bargain of a lifetime. In the end, only one taker got a brand new Mazda 626 at cost, all thanks to Jonathan Joseph Bowen.

The arrival of Jonathan filled a huge void in my life; I was ready to start afresh with my new little mate and work hard at getting it right. I didn't know anyone who was a good father and no one taught me how to be a father. I didn't do such a good job the first time round and I didn't want to blow it the second time around, so maybe Jonathan and I would learn from each other.

Isn't it strange how one of the biggest and most responsible jobs in life is parenthood, and yet so many of us cock it up? This time around, I was going for perfection and nothing less. At least if I fell short, it would still be a lot better than my first attempt.

The nightmares were getting less frequent by now and I was feeling a bit more comfortable on the same side of the street as a policeman, but only a bit. Maybe it was having responsibility that was giving me comfort in life. I was cherishing the role of parenthood and being in control of my own life. Who said little things don't matter because they do, I can assure you. The freedom to play guitar in my own home—amazing; not having to move out of the armchair for someone else, ie. my father-in-law. Even more amazing; not worrying about an alcoholic father coming home drunk, upsetting the home. Mind boggling; sleeping in a dry bed and having someone to love and comfort you when you're down. Priceless; that's how I was seeing life now. Anything else would be a bonus and, who knows, maybe that bonus might come in a forgiving letter from Serica's mum. I was only now beginning to realise that if five years of apologising wasn't enough then there was not much else I could do. I wrote my last letter to tell her again and for the last time:

Dear Mrs Mc—

Again I write to apologise and explain I genuinely and sincerely loved your daughter and never intended any hurt to come her way. It is only with hindsight that I realise the disgrace and shame and enormous pain I brought to Serica and yourself, and I can only again repeat I sincerely and genuinely loved your daughter and if you don't forgive me I'm sure God will, and I hope in time God will help you to deal with your pain as he's helping me deal with mine.
Yours sincerely,
Michael Bowen.
PS. I won't be writing again.

❀   ❀   ❀

And so now, I'm moving on with my life.

Poetry and songwriting were filling in my spare time to my enormous satisfaction. And, like everything in life, the more time you spend doing it, the better you get and, as a lot of people think, the luckier you get.

Poetry and songwriting were the windows to my soul and I sure was dressing up my window for all the world to see. My creative endeavours had become a wonderful soul-cleanser and, instead of carrying around the troubles of the past in my heart, I could hang them out to dry (so to speak) by sharing them with the world.

CHAPTER TWELVE

CALM SEAS

AS A FAMILY WE would regularly walk to the Mornington pier on weeknights, rain or shine. Fridays were special because we could buy freshly caught scallops, oysters and fish from the fishing trawlers moored at the pier. And Gurranabraher seemed a million miles away, not 13,000 miles.

I often closed my eyes and imagined with mixed emotions I was walking down Shandon Street or Patrick Street or even on The Strand in Youghal. And yet at times I didn't seem to have anywhere to run to and hide because I just wanted to cry for I missed being a child in Cork and I wanted Aunt Mary to hold me and tell me of all the good things in life where there's no heartaches and pain. I missed Breda holding my hand and pulling me along behind. I want to tell them how grateful I was to them for everything they did for me and how much I loved them; but this bastard macho world wouldn't allow me to and that made it worse. I wanted to see Stef's smiling face, my old mentor to whom I owe so much, and it broke my heart not to be able to see my beloved Cork Hibbs play.

The spectacular sights of Mornington were some compensation

for my longings for home, or maybe by now it should be called my for-
mer home. It was strange sitting in the middle, with the past of Ireland
in one hand and the future of Australia in the other. Both were pulling
at the strings of my heart, both had tragic histories and yet so different—so, so different. Both enormously beautiful. I really shouldn't
have been feeling so sad at the loss of leaving Ireland because it was
now five-years-plus since I arrived in Australia. I should have been
enormously grateful to have lived and loved in both countries. The
best of both worlds.

What an enormous experience of life, the best of the old world in
Ireland and it's magic and tragic history, and Australia, also with a
somewhat tragic past and an expected rosy future—one of the last
frontiers to yet see its full potential realised.

Growing up in the 1950s and 1960s in Ireland with an abundance
of local talent, and seeing all the great artists of the time who came to
Ireland (The Everly Brothers, Chubby Checker, The Searchers, The
Troggs, The Rolling Stones, Gordon Lightfoot, Roy Orbison, and The
Springfields, to name just a few). Helen and I were keeping the trend
going in Australia, I guess, just to keep in touch with the past. We went
to see my idol Ray Charles, Chris Kristofferson, Melanie, Dolly Parton,
and many more, as I was becoming more involved in music.

I have always viewed songs as milestones in our lives. Think about
it for a second . . . for example, the first time I heard The Byrds sing
'Mister Tamborine Man' it was 1965 and I was laying on the grass with
a portable radio in Youghal, County Cork. It was Radio Luxembourg
and they were playing the Top Twenty. I was amazed by the sound of
Roger McGuinn's twelve-string guitar. Where were you? The first time
I heard Ray Charles sing 'Take These Chains From My Heart' I was
dancing with Genie Mac in the Arcadia Ballroom in Cork in May,
1963. Every time I hear Glen Campbell sing 'Where's the Playground,
Susie?' or 'By the Time I Get to Phoenix' I am transported back to
Tralee and am outside Serica's door waiting to take her on a date. Every
time I hear 'Tie a Yellow Ribbon Round the Old Oak Tree' I don't think

of contra deals and Americans coming home, instead I'm dancing in the Brandon Hotel or at Horans.

I'm constantly amazed by the effect music has on us and how it transports us to a different place and time in our life. I wanted to experience this magic gift of being able to touch people in this way. The appetite to write more poetry and songs grew in me; I wanted to leave a legacy. When I die I want my children and their children's children to know who I am and what I was about. No doubt there will be things written about me and stories told, and if that is to be then it is better coming from me. After all, there is no one more qualified to talk about my own life than myself. There's a little bit of every writer in every song and a bit of the poet in his poetry.

Time moved on and my life was settling into Mr Average. But I knew in my heart of hearts that it was only for a period so I soaked up the tranquillity of Mr Average, doting on Jonathan, trying hard to be the perfect husband, perfect father and writing songs and poetry more than ever. I felt thankful to God every day for the amazing quality of life he bestowed on me and I suppose, like the prodigal son, God had given me a second chance. To this day, I'm so glad I picked Melbourne that morning in the office of British Airways. Thanks to Ronnie Dalany for winning his gold medal here in 1956, I feel as if I win a gold medal every day.

Aunt Mary would surely be proud and Stef would have a huge smile and say, 'Of course, I always knew you had it in you.' An excitement and confidence that I never felt before was growing inside me. But with every calm, comes a storm. Just when you think everything is quiet and normal, guess what?

I had a friend called Michael Hall who was a real estate agent (his people came from Athlone). He came to visit me one Sunday and took Helen and I to see a house in Wheelers Hill. Of course it was just to see. When Helen opened the door, she turned to Michael and said, 'How much is it?'

He replied, 'Do you like it?'

She shouted, 'It's just beautiful!'

'If you like it, you can afford it.'

So the next day we bought the house and made arrangements to move from our beloved Mornington, and all that fresh air and Friday night fish.

Within two months I had moved house and was on the move job-wise. TNT Transport was to be my new workplace as sales supervisor. The general manager there was also president of one of the Victorian Football League clubs. As a result, most of the sales staff were foot-ballers, and what a total disaster! By choice I would not have had any one of them on my staff. In fact, I wouldn't even allow them to sweep the floors. They were unreliable, inefficient, knew nothing about making sales and cared less, but they were footballers—trophies the GM liked to have around—much to the detriment of TNT. I can only imagine the enormous amount of money the company wasted; Sir Peter Ables must have lost a lot as a result. It was an impossible task for me to try to make those guys efficient and accountable. So after eighteen months I had had enough and was head-hunted by a company which was in receivership: Finemores Transport in Wagga Wagga, NSW (also known as 'the place of the crows' to the Aborigines).

I spent a wonderful period of time there helping them out of receivership doing everything from getting them storage facilities in Melbourne to canvassing every business in Wagga Wagga—and I mean every one. I organised truckloads from city to city, criss-crossing the country. Finemores had mainly been freighting livestock and got into trouble due to the drought and subsequent shortage of livestock in Australia, so it was my primary job to help them to move over to dry freight and general freight where there were more opportunities for such a large transport company.

The travelling was very demanding and tiring. Of course there were plenty of chemicals—nod nod, wink wink—to help you not be so tired. I never took up that opportunity (thankfully), but I knew a few who did and you won't be reading any of their biographies.

I was missing the stable life of home and Jonathan—by far my best mate. So with a job well done, and with a generous bonus cheque, I returned to a stable family life in Wheelers Hill. After a well-earned break, I set out to look after and manage Danny Hewitt's recently acquired Motor Sales in Hallam, and to the astonishing news that Jonathan was about to have a brother or sister. I thought I was the luckiest person in the world considering the doctor told us after Jonathan's birth that the chances of another child were a thousand to one. This child was breaking all the rules and certainly was going to be special. Emmett Michael's arrival on 31 October 1983, at Glen Waverley Private Hospital, was a far cry from the North Infirmary Hospital in Cork where his father spent most of his youth.

Emmett Michael announced himself to the world with a huge scream and then lay in his delightful mother's arms with a beautiful smile on his face reflecting the smiles on his proud mum and dad. Guess who thought he had the two best looking kids in Australia?

Isn't life strange and also magic when you think about it? One day, you're running around Gurranabraher with patches in your trousers and not a morsel of food on the table to eat. Then, in what seems like the blink of an eye, you're married and have children and your life is totally different. And then, in what seems like no time at all, life turns you upside down or is it love that turns you upside down? And in no compromised fashion, I might add. Here I was in Australia living the perfect life in anyone's language: a good job, a lovely home, the perfect wife, and two gorgeous children, all healthy and a dry bed. How different life is now!

I was hoping life was being as good to Niall and Liz and all those I loved in Ireland. I was coming to terms more with my own responsibilities. I now accepted for the first time since I left Ireland I had not been as understanding to Mary as I should have been. But then again, Ireland in a way bred into us males an element of macho arrogance and I was beginning to understand more of my own inadequacies in coping with life. Gone long ago was my sense that life only shat on me and, in its place, I had an understanding that you only get out of life what you put in. On reflection, I didn't put much into my relationship with Mary and maybe if I had, she might have been more confident about the marriage. Who knows? My views on lots of things were certainly softening.

If I was honest with Serica, who knows what the outcome might have been? Though honesty certainly didn't pay in the case of Marion in Limerick, when I nearly got my head shot off. So much for honesty. I can say in my heart of hearts, I never intended any disrespect or harm to anyone even in my wild, promiscuous spree, as I looked back ten years later.

Speaking of the blink of an eye, ten years had gone and in two more years I would be able to return to Ireland. I said life was strange and magic, well, what do you know? Helen and I attended a St Patrick's Day dinner in the Moonee Ponds Hall and there I saw Marion Maloney, Serica's best friend. I was gob-smacked. I thought, *What game is God playing with me now, just when I thought life was normal? He is now going to throw it upside down again, oh no!*

'Michael,' Marion shouted out. 'Oh, Jesus Christ, I don't believe it! Michael Bowen.' No words would come out of my mouth. I wiped tears from my eyes and when speech finally came to me after the hugging I asked, 'How is she?' 'Not good, Michael, not good at all.' My heart ached with the news. I took Marion and introduced her to Helen and she introduced us to her husband, Eamon. We agreed to meet on Monday and she would give me all the news.

Monday finally arrived and I was all ears for Marion. She told me Serica married the local bank manager and had three daughters and she was not in good health as he beat her a lot. He constantly threatened to take the children away from her. I was furious as to why life had dealt her such a hand. Such a gorgeous, gentle lady didn't deserve a break like that.

'How many times do I have to say life is strange, Marion? It's OK for a brute like that to abuse a beautiful lady like her, and it was wrong for me to love her—how stupid can that be, Marion? How stupid!' I cried. 'Marion, I must have written hundreds of letters to her mum apologising and telling her how much I loved Serica and not one reply, not one.'

'I know, Michael. Her mum showed my mum all the letters, but neither one told Serica, and now I'm sorry I didn't tell her either.'

'Oh my God, Marion, how could they have let this happen to my beautiful Serica? How could they? I loved her so much and I would have done anything for her. Isn't life a bitch? God, I get so confused with it sometimes. Marion, what can I do for her? Is there anything I can do to make life better for her?'

'I don't think so, Michael, but I will write to her during the week and let her know I met with you.'

Six hours of catching up just flew and I was so grateful to Marion for her honesty and fairness towards me. She was most understanding. Marion agreed to come over to visit Helen and I on Sunday and bring Eamon and her daughter for a barbecue. Again, I couldn't wait for Sunday to catch up on more news and, of course, I was on the phone each day to Marion getting additional snippets. Why, oh, why, I wondered . . . and what brought Marion and I together after all those years?

There I was after ten years of self-exile, working hard to put my life into some normality and settle down. For the first time in my life, I was happy in myself and with my family and God confronted me with the most disturbing issue of my past. Was it an omen? Was it a challenge? Was it a reminder of true love? I honestly couldn't tell. All I knew was I was totally confused and was concerned for everyone involved in the situation.

Still a million questions running around in my head: *Why, oh why in God's name would anyone want to abuse such a beautiful lady?* Whoever he was, he must have been unstable and certainly ungrateful for the privilege of having that wonderful woman to share his life with, a lady that anyone in their right mind would kill for. I could only conclude that whoever he was, the ungrateful bastard was not in his right mind.

He must have got a slap in the head too many times with a hurley.

It wasn't fair to me and to those around me and those whom I loved that God confronted me with so much emotion. I can't remember how many times I've said, 'Isn't life strange?' Just when you think everything is hunky-dory and every square peg in life fits into a square hole, the bloody wheel falls off the wagon of life, or the damn donkey that pulls it dies. The road you set out on is never the one you end the journey on and, up to now, my whole life is a testimony to this.

So the question then was: where is this road going to take me and will it be more heartache and pain, not just for me alone, but also for those who are precious to me and whom I love dearly? My heart of hearts was telling me I was again about to take a journey through the valley of tears.

I had been down that road so many times I knew every bend. Hopefully God would be kinder to me and to those around me this time. I felt more mature—or at least I thought I was—and I felt I could take the consequences on the chin. I guess it was as the crims say: if you do the crime, be prepared to do the time. But it was my family I feared for and, if there were any consequences, it might have hurt them. To be truthful, Serica's situation was uppermost in my thoughts. In God's name, how can you love someone emphatically and then when you get news that they are being abused in such a manner, you are not moved? You wouldn't be human if you didn't feel anything.

Rather than wait for Marion and family to arrive on Sunday by cab, I drove to Northcote to pick them up, and got another hour of chitchat. Unashamedly, I questioned Marion on everything about Serica, and again she was wonderfully gracious in her replies. It didn't seem to bother Helen at all; the fact that the whole afternoon's conversation was Serica and Tralee. It was magic to hear the true Tralee accent and so much about my favourite town.

Then, as if to prove a point that life is strange, no sooner did Marion come into my life, than she was departing from it. Just as I picked up the keys of my car to drive them home after what was a wonderful get-ting-to-know-one-another day, she told us they were returning to Tralee in three months time for a six-month-visit and then were mov-ing permanently to the United States.

Again I asked myself what game was God playing with me. Was Marion the messenger of sad tidings? I was lost. I just didn't know. What did it all mean? As Marion and Eamon thanked Helen for a won-derful day, I looked to the heavens and whispered, 'You're the puppet master and you're pulling the strings this time and I guess I will have to dance to whatever tune you play for me. So, JC, I'm in your hands.'

Prior to Marion and Eamon's departure to Ireland, Marion kept in touch regularly to update me on Serica's health and wellbeing. And it cut me inside when on one occasion she told me Serica's husband locked her in a shed in her backyard. I was furious with God—how could he allow this in good old Catholic Ireland? I just couldn't imag-ine her crime. I felt useless and enormously angry because I couldn't help. Sometimes life's a bitch, and that's what I thought of it then. Ireland was again proving to be a country stuck in a time of secrets.

Clifford Davis paid me a surprise visit at work the next day (what did I say about life being strange!). I hadn't seen Clifford for years, and boy-oh-boy was I shocked when he offered to take me to dinner and pay me back the monies I lent him for his airfare when he migrated ten years ago. After I received my cheque, I ate as much as I could and drank everything that Clifford bought for me. He then took me to his office—obviously to impress me—and showed me his new lifestyle and wealth.

Then, in typical Irish cynical manner, he said, 'You know you're a fuckin' idiot.' I calmly asked him to explain, thinking I should have killed him first. He handed me some documents to read: it was his salary and commission statement. I was numb. The only words that would come out of my mouth were, 'Fuck, how many people a year do you have to knock off to get this enormous amount of money? Christ, you could buy all of Gurranabraher with that.'

'You're right,' he told me, 'And you know what? You could earn that and more if you were doing what I'm doing because you're one of the best salespeople I know,' hence the backhanded compliment.

I went home to consider my professional future. Clifford was right: I was a fuckin' idiot. I didn't understand my self-worth. I was a good salesperson—more than good—and I definitely had a better way with, and an understanding of, people than Clifford. And if Clifford could earn that amount of money, surely I could do better. So exactly one week later, I started in the insurance and investment world with AMP, Australia's biggest life insurance office.

Clifford was right—I was good—and for the next two years I went about building a wonderful business and lifestyle. It gave me the opportunity to spend lots of time with the family and develop my music and poetry skills. Life was so good. I thought I was living in heaven, and I was amazed I found time for things like washing Jonathan and Emmett and taking them to school and kindergarten, and absolutely loving every minute of it. On many occasions, I would spend all day at kindy with them. I loved playing mum, and during that time the seed of a very strong bond was sown with the children.

In spite of Clifford's newfound wealth, he never learned how to control the monkey on his back, and for that reason I stayed out of his way most of the time, although I did have the odd drink with him now and again, for old time's sake. Second time around, I was much wiser and didn't take any shit.

As my time of self-exile would be up soon, I grew anxious. I had promised that I would be back in Ireland as soon as the twelve years were up and I decided I was going to fulfil my promise. Twelve years is a long time to wait to see those you love. For over a year I had had butterflies in my stomach—a lot of things happen over such a long time.

One of the sad tasks Helen and I would have to do when we got back was to visit our friend Eireen and her two daughters. My old mate John had died after they returned to Ireland. As Eireen explained in her letter, winning the lottery could sometimes cost you a lot more I would miss having that promised drink with him in his local in Mayfield and teasing him over the rented shoes.

Sadly, I wouldn't see my nan either as she died at the ripe age of 99. What a life of fulfilment she had: a real character, a no-nonsense woman, as hard as a rock and as soft as a tissue. She loved her drop of whiskey and snuff. She was the matriarch of the family, and my Aunt Mary was a carbon copy. Obviously it was in the genes.

I could just see Aunt Mary with her big smile and tears running down her face just wanting to squeeze and hug me and then standing tall and saying, 'What did I tell you, boy? I'm so proud of you.' I was willing to bet a million dollars that's what she'd say word for word. And then she would go on and ask me about my health and comment on what a gorgeous wife and children I have, and the prodigal nephew would be welcomed back with open arms and no strings attached. That's why God made Mary so special—to comfort the likes of me, no questions asked. She just couldn't help but treat me like a king every time I came into contact with her. How lucky was I to be loved by someone like her, a true living angel and she was my angel, all to myself. Thank you, God.

And what of Serica? What would I do? Would I go to Tralee to find out what might have been? And if so, what would her reaction be? Would she be willing to see me, and if she did, then what? Would all the emotions come flooding back? How would I cope? I was sure my emotions would surface, even after twelve years, I had no doubt they would.

For God's sake, I had only to turn on the radio and hear Glen Campbell's 'Where's the Playground, Susie?' or Tony Orlando's 'Tie a Yellow Ribbon Round the Old Oak Tree' or Charlie Rich's 'The Most Beautiful Girl in the World' and I was already in the palm of her hand. I needed to know that she wasn't in danger from her aggressive, over-bearing husband and that she was well. Even if I went to Tralee and I didn't see her, I knew enough people who could let me know if she was OK. I was sure they would have put their prejudices behind them after twelve years and maybe I would get the opportunity to front Serica senior and let her see I was a better person for the experience of selfishness and inconsideration shown to her and Serica twelve years ago. Again, I would let her know I sincerely loved her daughter. I would take it on the chin, whatever she might say, and I would expect the wrath of God. But I hoped, like me, she would have mellowed with time. I sincerely hoped so.

I was hoping it was a time for healing in Ireland.

I felt I should also find time while in Ireland to visit Marion in Limerick to try to reconcile with her father, considering I was only a second away from meeting my maker. Maybe he might also have mellowed over the years, and why not? Without a doubt, Marion was the most mellow, quiet and pleasant lady you would ever wish to meet. Come to think of it—except for the one occasion where he wanted to shoot me—her father was a very gentle soul, as was her mum.

I got goose pimples when I thought of Stef seeing me after twelve years. Virtually word for word he would say to me, 'Fuck, Michael, I can't leave you alone for five minutes without you getting into trouble,' and he would be beaming at me. Time meant nothing between us, whether it was five minutes or a hundred years. We were like Siamese twins, joined at the hearts, forever best friends and that won't even change when we are in our graves. I am so grateful to him for so much.

My heart would sink in my chest the minute Breda hugged me and held my hand. It would bring back so many memories: the cold nights we huddled together so she could keep me warm. We thought we were the only two lost souls on earth. All the times she walked me to the City Hall in the rain for medical checks to monitor my pneumonia and bronchitis, of course, we had no money for the bus for if we had we would have spent it on food anyway. Also, I remember the rounds of convents begging for food and clothes.

The guilt I felt about the times Aunt Mary took me to her house to stay and left Breda behind to be physically, mentally and sexually abused by a drunken father weighed on me heavily. I had failed to understand or do anything about it as a child, and maybe now I might be able to give her some comfort in return for all she did for me.

Terrible to think Liza and Aunt Mary were aware of this abuse occurring and failed to do anything about it. Rather, they were ashamed and guilt-ridden, and therefore ridiculed her rather than defended her—a sure sign of guilt. And in my heart I knew this was an issue that she and she alone would have to confront in her own time, but it sure explained why for years I had been getting regular reverse-charge phone calls from a very depressed and intoxicated sister, costing me thousands of dollars.

I failed to understand the full extent of her abuse, but how could I fully understand it? I think you only understand when you are the victim, otherwise it is unbelievable for anyone other than that person to really know what it's like. I could only try to comfort her and I wasn't even sure that would be enough. All I can say now is God forgive those who sin against children for if parents sin against their own flesh and blood, who can they be trusted with if not their own?

Children are the most precious gift given to us from God—a privilege—and sadly, they are so often abused. But, as I have said, it was a time of secrets. The clergy also failed to act and support the victims on many occasions. For they were wary as they had their own catalogue of secrets that are only now being revealed. Breda's secret was in my heart and I would have to hold onto it until she was ready to share it.

Would Niall be as tall as me, and fair-haired like me, or dark like Mary? How would he react? Would he be curious and want to know about the missing years and why Mary and I broke up? Would he want to know all the details of our split and would he question me on my infidelities. Would he understand? Would he want to understand or would his mind be prejudiced to the good old Irish religious views of life? Or had enough time passed to allow him to see a broader view of life? I hoped so. I made my mind up to answer any questions he may have for me truthfully because I was sure he had heard lots of stories over the years about me and when I met him it might be my only chance to clarify everything.

And the same went for Liz, for she may want to know all too. Of course, they might also not want to see me at all and I would have to deal with the disappointment of that. And yet Jonathan and Emmett were utterly bursting with excitement·at the thought of meeting their half-brother and half-sister: different views from different sides of the world to the same problem. And because we would be in good old Catholic Ireland, Helen would no doubt have to put up the snide remarks of being 'the other woman'. But we were well prepared for that as I wouldn't allow that to happen; no woman who walks into my life is lesser because of me.

On the good side, there was Helen's family to meet (almost half of Galway) and there was the hurling and football to see. There was Dublin and Wicklow to be reacquainted with, an abundance of scenery, good pubs and sing-a-longs, and plenty of opportunities to try out my new songs.

I felt good enough about my standard of songwriting, I wanted to talk to the people at Radio Telefis Eireann (Ireland's national television and radio broadcasting authority) regarding the rules of entry for the National Song Contest. I had always wanted to see if I could write a song for the competition that had a good chance of winning. After all, it's Ireland's forerunner to the Eurovision Song Contest and I had held a longing to have an involvement in that major European event. I had promised myself the rewards of success would influence people and I was going to have an impact on Eurovision in no small way . . . only time would tell if my promise would bear fruit.

Why Eurovision? Because it's one of the biggest TV music programs in the world and sometimes reaches an audience of up to one billion people. I promised myself I was going to have an impact on this event in one way or another.

As time approached for my return, always the question lingered: what might have been? If Mary had set up home with just me and the children; if she had seen a doctor about her bed-wetting problem; if I got to tell Serica about my marriage problems; if Marion's dad hadn't threatened to shoot me; if Mick had taken up the offers to be a professional football player; if they had let me join the school band; if Stef hadn't taken the time to groom me to be a good salesman; if Liza had not been sick so often; if Aunt Mary wasn't my angel and my cornerstone; if I didn't come to Australia; if Ron Dalany didn't win the mile in 1956; if I didn't meet Bob Dallas. If . . . if . . . if. A million ifs—how would my life be different?

Isn't it strange how your life can be changed by one 'if only'? We have to accept that our lives are constantly changing and you can look at it negatively or positively. My present conclusion is that I'm blessed, I must be the luckiest guy on earth. I have an education from the University of Life, with top honours. I have experienced an abundance of love, I have known poverty as if it were my twin brother and now I know what it's like to be able to go anywhere in the world and not have to look in the bank book first to know what's there. I know what it's like to have nothing but sheep's head soup on Sunday for dinner, and I know what it's like to have caviar and champagne and so much more.

My aunt was right: you might be born in shit but you don't have to live in it. Life is a wonderful gift from God and it should be lived and not wasted. Too many people accept the station they are born into. I assume they are like that because of their background, they believe they cannot progress. Of course they can! When God created this world he didn't say it was for the chosen few now did he? No. He said it was for all to share. All we have to do is step up and take our share but no, we don't do that! We stand back humbly and let others go first, that's so we don't look selfish or greedy, that's what you did in my hometown in the 1950s.

We were badly educated, we were taught to be humble and dull and not spontaneous or exciting. I recall my first day at school when the teacher fixed her gaze on two students, 'Sit down there, Johnny and Mary, don't be smart and shut up.' For God's sake, that's exactly why we were going to school: to learn how to be smart! No wonder I was so frustrated in school in the limited time I spent there. I now understand why on my final day at school I couldn't read or write. No one recognised I was dyslexic. Life was all about knowing your place in society and not being smart. We were never encouraged to move beyond our social standing and now I feel so sorry for so many smart lads I went to school with because the teacher didn't see they had wings and could fly. I felt they were deprived of a better quality of life and, here we go again with the 'what ifs'.

I have since learned that the only thing that makes a difference to your life as to whether you live in poverty or wealth is one word: Attitude. Your Attitude, and don't you forget it. No matter where you come from or what your background is, don't let anyone tell you otherwise, even my Aunt Mary knew that.

So when I journeyed to Ireland I did so with my head held high and I felt six feet tall, even though I'm five foot ten. No, I wasn't going backward, I was going forward, looking for answers to what might have been and building a new relationship with Ireland and all those I left behind in 1974. I would never look back again, only forward, and I would accept whatever challenges lay before me (not problems, my days of problems and nightmares were over), and a new day would dawn when I touched down at Shannon Airport.

CHAPTER THIRTEEN

MENDING BRIDGES

STEPPING ON BOARD the 747 jumbo plane at Tullarmarine Airport, bound for London, I was both excited and scared. The prodigal son was returning, to what reception I did not know.

I spent most of the journey writing poetry, which would form part of my first published book of poems titled, *Window to My Soul*. I comforted Emmett who was having difficulties with his ears caused by the high altitude. Jonathan was being a typical curious six year old, talking to all the other passengers and winning the hearts of the air hostesses. Helen seemed to take the flight in her stride.

On reaching London we had to change to an Aer Lingus flight to travel on to Shannon. The four of us were pretty much exhausted, but the adrenaline kicked in as soon as we saw the green Aer Lingus plane that was taking us to Shannon. All fear was well and truly gone, I felt only excitement and anticipation at putting my feet on home soil once more. It was an entirely different feeling to the last time I was in London. Tears were running down my cheeks, I couldn't contain my joy. I was actually crying and laughing at once, and I hadn't even stepped on the plane yet. The last leg of the twelve-year journey to reach home—Cork, in mother Ireland—was about to end.

The Aer Lingus crew were just marvellous to Helen and the children considering the long journey we had just endured. They were most inquisitive about Australia and wanted to know what was happening in the Aussie TV soap, *Neighbours*. Jonathan and Emmett were given the full run of the plane by the crew and I would not have been surprised if they had let Jonathan land the plane in Shannon! It was typical Irish hospitality and they were giving us the red carpet treatment. A nicer welcome home I could not have wished for.

Ireland never looked lovelier in the cape of green she wore to welcome home her prodigal son. I'm lost for words to describe the feeling I had as I kissed the ground upon putting my feet on the tarmac. Twelve years of my life flashed in front of me in one second. The children were confused: every time they looked at me, all they saw were tears and more tears.

We rushed through customs, picked up our bags and I swear to God I thought the entire population of Galway turned up there to meet us. I was expecting to be lifted up onto someone's shoulders and carried about! I swear Christy Ring didn't get this sort of treatment when he won his many all-Ireland medals with the Cork hurling team. I was overwhelmed by the jubilation of the new relatives and extended family. Everything was a haze until someone said, 'Jaysus lads, hurry up and let's go for a pint.'

Ennis was designated as the place I would have my first pint of Guinness in Ireland in twelve years, and not too soon for me I can tell you. It tasted like honey of the gods. I savoured every drop. And many more pints were drank before we got to Galway. Helen's family were just a wonderful bunch of joyful, hospitable people with not one sign of prejudice towards me considering I was a previously married man. Just wonderful people. However, prejudice did finally raise its ugly head in the form of Helen's best mate—another Helen—who was only too happy every time the opportunity came her way to make a snide remark and show her ignorance and narrow-minded thinking.

But then again, she was rather surprisingly snipey towards Helen also. I decided not to react to her jibes and let the ball go through to the keeper (a good old Aussie expression).

Time was flying by us with so much to catch up on. I decided to visit Tralee for the Rose of Tralee Festival on my own, to do some writing and look for some answers. I left the family in Trim—the home of Helen's sister—for four days. I drove to Tullamore where I picked up a hitchhiker who was going to Limerick and we chatted all the way. He was genuinely astonished when I told him I was on my way to Tralee after leaving Trim earlier that morning. 'All that way in one day, you're kidding,' he gasped. I smiled and nodded, 'Yep.' And I found myself saying, 'Just a cruise for an Aussie, son.' 'Fucking mad,' he replied and we both laughed.

The Limerick to Tralee leg of the journey was like the clock had stopped twelve years ago, and in many respects it had. I knew every inch of the road. I swanned through Newcastle West, Abbeyfeale, Castleisland, then the last few miles into Tralee and I could hear those words again, 'I'm only a heartbeat away from my beloved Tralee.'

My heart began to beat faster. The graveyard was on my right with its large cross dedicated to the fallen IRA heroes. I pushed the cassette into the slot in the dashboard and Glen Campbell sang 'Where's the Playground, Susie?' and I arrived at Horans. I stopped outside and my mind was instantly cast back to 1973. I leant over the steering wheel and caught my breath for a minute and tried to take it all in, but I was in a state of disbelief that I had actually made it back. It was like being in a dream and I was expecting to wake up any minute. I pinched myself and, yes, I was awake, still sitting outside Horans in the car, and Glen Campbell was singing 'By the Time I get to Phoenix'. I wonder if Jimmy Webb could have written a song, 'By the Time I get to Melbourne and Back'.

'Excuse me, could you kindly guide me to where the Brandon Hotel is, please?' a lady with an American accent asked me. I cordially obliged, to which she replied, 'For a local, you have a strange accent, but it's nice.' I smiled and accepted her comment as a compliment.

I leant on the counter and asked for a Double Diamond. Sorry sir, no Double Diamond, try a Heineken—it kills Double Diamond. No Jim and no familiar surrounds or faces. I finished my drink and left disappointed as they had no vacancies either. I pulled up outside the Grand Hotel and hoped there had been a change of management. If not, I might have had to sleep in the car, and I didn't fancy that. I approached reception and declared, 'Bowen's the name, from Australia. Melbourne, Australia.' I bluffed that I had a booking, made some months ago, for three nights. The receptionist looked confused as she scanned the booking list for my name.

I told her to keep an eye on my bag as I fought my way to the bar for a drink. I was halfway through my pint when she approached. 'Mr Bowen, your room's now ready.' I was astonished as the hotels were usually booked out during the festival. I slipped her a fiver and we were both happy. At least I knew I had a bed for the next few nights, so what if it was on my own? I had no plans other than to enjoy good music and do some writing.

Thank God, there must have been a change in management there for if there hadn't, and anyone remembered the events of my last stay there, I would have had no hope of getting a room in that fine historic establishment. Maybe they didn't recognise me with my clothes on, I sniggered to myself. I took the last slug of my pint of Heineken and took my bags to my room. I looked in the bathroom mirror, as I had many times before in the very same room, only this time the face that looked back at me was twelve years older. I closed my eyes for a moment and wondered when I opened them again would I see the old me back from 1973 and '74, and would everything that has happened between then and now be just a dream? I opened my eyes to confirm—no dream.

I wandered off down past The Brogue Inn to Houlihans Lounge Bar in Rock Street. But before I entered I couldn't help but stare over once again at The Brogue where so many memories were made. I was sure to any onlooker it must look like I'd just stuck my finger in a light socket for I felt my hair standing on end and my body was covered in goose pimples. I realised I was blocking the entrance to Houlihans so in I went.

I ordered a pint of Heineken from an unsuspecting Francie Houlihan who, upon delivering the perfect pint, smiled as I handed him a ten-pound note. He said, 'You remind me of someone.' I said, 'Yes, why don't you ask your brother, Richie?' who was also behind the bar serving.

'Jesus Christ, Francie, that's what's-his-name who was going out with what's-her-name,' Richie shouted.

'Holy Mother of God, what are you doing here?'

'I'm visiting, looking for answers, and writing,' I responded. 'Richie, how's Serica?' I enquired.

'Ah, sure, we don't see a lot of her nowadays. You know she's married?'

'Yes, I know and I also heard she's not well.'

'Sure, there are always rumours going around Tralee, as you know.'

'Yes, I heard them as far away as Australia.'

'Ah, sure, you never know,' was his reply.

We exchanged stories of Australia and our respective families over another few pints. Sadly, I wouldn't be seeing Serica's mum as I learnt she had passed away some time ago. I left Richie smiling with some Australian t-shirts I gave him for his children. I did a pub crawl through all the old haunts and finished up playing guitar and singing for a group of American tourists back at the Grand Hotel. In a strange way, I felt I was giving the hotel back something for the inconvenience I caused all those years ago.

I was flattered when the hotel manager bought me a pint and thanked me for entertaining his patrons. Oh, how the wheel turns! And for the first time in my life, I actually declined, not one but two offers of bed companions for the night. And for the first time in many years, I was actually proud of my behaviour. Again, dare I say, oh how the wheel turns . . .

I headed off early next morning to my heaven-on-earth, the site of the movie, *Ryan's Daughter* in Slay Head, Dun Chaoin. It was absolutely bucketing down as I made my way out along the rugged coast to my destination. Visibility was to a minimum, but who cared when you were in heaven? I had waited twelve years to write in that schoolhouse and no amount of rain was going to stop me. Out of the car, over the ditch, up the small brow of a hill and there it was—the original schoolhouse especially built for the movie, I didn't mind if it wasn't a hundred or two hundred years old, it was the whole thing of the movie I loved and it was my turn to soak up the atmosphere of it. It was still bucketing down and I was soaked to the skin but I didn't care as I made my way down to the schoolhouse on the edge of the cliffs.

The inhospitable Atlantic winds and rain had taken their toll on the building, as had the souvenir hunters. It was only a shell of what it had been. I sank into the only corner of the building where no rain was coming in to pour my heart out and complete my mission of writing, *Window to My Soul.*

For two days, I sat huddled in the wind-swept corner and reached into my heart for all the emotion I could find in relentless rain and cold. Finally, mission accomplished. I felt an even stronger affinity with the area.

I reacquainted myself with some of the locals in Tralee before I left to head back to Trim and I was saddened by the stories I heard about Serica—someone I loved so much—and the cruelty that had become a part of her life. I was reluctant to go and see her for fear that she may suffer ramifications as a result of my visit. Now that I could return to Ireland as often as I liked, I felt there would be an more opportune time in the future to bring a conclusion to that particular piece of unfinished business.

As happy as a pig in shit is a good old Irish saying and it describes how I felt as I made my way back to Trim to pick up Helen and the children. From there, we journeyed to Dublin and then onto Wicklow's Glendalough to take in some sightseeing before we got to Cork.

Helen and I decided to book into a hotel rather than stay with Liza and Mick. We felt Liza was still iffy about Helen and still treated her as 'the other woman', and I was not going to stand for Helen being treated that way. By staying in a hotel, it gave us greater control over our movements and therefore any time we felt uncomfortable we could just leave. We didn't put a time limit on our stay, we had a 'let's see how we go' attitude.

My expectations of everyone's welcome were spot on: Breda's tears and hugs; Aunt Mary had more tears; Stef's 'Fuck, boy'; Liza's snipes; and Mick, well, Mick was Mick—now very easygoing in his retirement and bearing only a slight reflection of his youthful good looks. Mick was a much more subdued man than the man I hardly knew as a child, but I was curious to get to know him even better now. I had learned to forgive and not be judgmental about the past. I felt there was no point having a chip on my shoulder: chips only bring heartaches for everyone and never resolve anything. I was only looking for answers and hopefully to mend some bridges.

Breda organised for me to meet with Niall at her home on my second day in Cork. I was scared and happy at the same time. *What a strange feeling to have,* I thought. I wasn't quite sure how to react. Niall was cautious too: quiet with a very gentle nature. We shook hands and then embraced, our conversation was mainly about his interest in music and soccer and I was most impressed with his knowledge on both subjects. The Police was his favourite group and Liverpool was his favourite team.

He told me his mum was well and Elizabeth was doing fine at school. He humbly apologised that Elizabeth did not want to meet with me and I assured him I understood. We agreed to meet the next day at his work for a few minutes so he could see Jonathan—his new half-brother. I left feeling very proud and I told him to tell his mum she did a wonderful job in raising him to be such a lovely young man. We also agreed to meet again on my return the following year, and hopefully spend more time together.

I was happy with the result of both meetings and knew in my heart mending bridges was a slow, cautious job and only time would tell. Helen and I were saddened when we visited Eireen and the children because with John gone, I wouldn't get to fulfil my promise of sharing a few pints with him in his local. The remainder of the following three days in Cork was spent reacquainting myself with old friends and showing Helen and the children the local sights, of which I was very proud. I wanted to see The Cork Opera House considering my fond memories of all the wonderful nights I had there and, of course, I couldn't miss the opportunity of having one more look around The Arcadia Ballroom—the 'Arc', as it was called in my days—where I spent so many of my Saturday and Sunday nights dancing to wonderful bands that worked very hard for their money. Cork audiences wouldn't tolerate second-rate talent and I can assure you Jim Reeves of 'He'll Have to Go' fame soon found out when they booed him out of town.

Cork hadn't changed much in my twelve-year exile and I was happy it hadn't for I was now seeing it with fresh eyes and I liked what I saw. I must say, I was most concerned when told of the drug problem among the young in my city of birth and held fears for the future. I knew most cities around the world had a drug problem but I had been seeing Cork through rose-coloured glasses and, when I fully understood the situation, I feared for the young of the future if the problem wasn't addressed immediately. I made my feelings public in *Window to My Soul*.

After many more kisses and hugs and 'I told you so's' from Aunt Mary, and many more kisses and tears and 'I'll miss me brother,' from Breda, along with guaranteeing our lifelong friendship with my mentor, Stef, and lots and lots of 'Fuck, boy' and a final goodbye to Mick and Liza, we departed with the assurance that I would return again the following year.

Helen, the children and I headed for Galway but not before I took them to see my heaven-on-earth in Slay Head so I could share the magic of the place with them. It was certainly worth going there again, just to see the look in Jonathan's eyes when he saw the schoolhouse. He, like me, just fell in love with the place instantly. Jonathan sat on my lap in the corner where only nine days previously I had been writing and I just loved sharing all the poems and stories with him. Yeah, I was in my seventh heaven.

We returned to Galway to celebrate Jonathan's seventh birthday, which he was delighted to be spending in Ireland. Our remaining time in Galway was mainly spent visiting Helen's friends and family, drinking and singing new songs. Helen's brother got me a ticket for the All Ireland hurling final, Cork vs. Galway. I had to travel with a load of Galway lads to the game. I was hoping Galway would win and everyone could celebrate the week away. Yes, everyone celebrated for a week alright, even though Cork won the final. God help us if Galway had won, I'm sure the celebrations would have run for a month. Even though they lost, the Galwegians refused to let it dampen their spirits and, boy-oh-boy, can they party!

The day for leaving and returning to Australia came much too soon for us and we were really saddened to be leaving Ireland. Except this time there was a difference. I knew I would be back the next year and that thought gave me comfort as I still had bridges to mend and more answers to find. We bid our farewells to friends and family with cases of presents and, having drunk more than my fair share of Heineken and Guinness, we headed for the land of Oz—as Australia is fondly known around the world.

❀   ❀   ❀

The twelve months that followed our return were very successful from a business point of view as I hit my stride. Jonathan was cruising at school and Emmett at pre-school. Life was easy and comfortable for the Bowens. Christmas came and went with the same rituals, and it soon came to pass that it was time again to go to Ireland. Except this time I was travelling on my own for Helen and the children were staying in Oz. This time, I decided to fly into Cork.

No butterflies when I stepped onto the jumbo, just a wonderful feeling of expectation. I knew in my heart and soul that it was going to be OK. I was not going backwards, I was visiting and then I would be returning home to Oz. I liked the idea of calling Oz home, after all, why not? That was where I was earning my living and paying my taxes.

I find it enormously comforting and therapeutic writing when flying, particularly since the flights take so long travelling to Europe. The writing keeps me preoccupied so I don't get too woossie thinking of those I've left behind. Writing seems to come to me, almost like a second nature, once I step onto an airplane—a great, comforting companion in flight, and a wonderful way to pass time. It must have something to do with being nearer to heaven (at least that's my explanation).

After a stop in Hong Kong to refuel, and a change of carriers in London, I was on an Aer Lingus flight heading to Cork. *Strange,* I was thinking to myself, as we approached land, *all the times Eugene Buckley and myself came out to the old airport, Farmer's Cross, just to look at the aeroplanes, (me with patches in the arse of my pants), and now it's a lifetime away from all that poverty.* My my, how life changes. Yes, Gurranabraher was so good to me in shaping my destiny.

I kissed the ground under my feet as soon as I touched the tarmac and I felt privileged to be able to fly into my place of birth. Breda was jumping up and down with excitement when I stepped out from customs and, just like the old days, she took me by the hand. But this time she lead me to the bar for what would become my ritual: a customary 'welcome home' pint of Heineken.

My time was spent with Liza and Mick, Breda and her wonderful husband, Tim (a more gentle and understanding man you will never meet). Breda's three sons, Tim, David and Kevin, were a lovely bunch of young lads. Niall occasionally joined us for a few drinks in the evenings at the local and slowly bridges were mending.

I sometimes sat outside Elizabeth's school in my hired car, just to get a glimpse of what she looked like. I was reluctant to intrude on her privacy as she requested she didn't want to meet with me, but surely that didn't mean that I couldn't look at her from a distance . . . it didn't stop me from feeling like a stalker, however. Elizabeth looked like a wonderful young lady and I couldn't help feeling humbled by the great job her mum did in raising her.

Somehow I plucked up the courage to ring Serica in Tralee and I was astonishingly surprised that she agreed to meet with me. I parked just down from the Brandon Hotel and waited nervously in anticipation. I pushed Glen Campbell's cassette into the slot and pinched myself as soon as he sang 'Where's the Playground, Susie?' I struggled to hold back the tears. I felt privileged and blessed to be given the opportunity to perhaps complete unfinished business.

No stars in heaven ever shone that bright and that was how she looked. Time made no difference in this girl's life, in spite of her hardships. She was still radiant with a wonderful smile and a twinkle in her eye.

We drove to Killarney so none of the locals would see us together and, in a wonderfully quaint pub over many drinks, we exchanged stories of the last thirteen years. Serica explained the great loss she felt when her mum passed away some years prior. I was deeply saddened to hear Serica was not informed of the many times I wrote to Serica senior apologising for my deceitful conduct.

'Serica, I must have written hundreds of letters to her explaining, and you were never informed?' My heart just sank with sadness. But this was a time of mending, not of opening old wounds. After Serica explained to the barman that we were on our honeymoon, we headed to the car park of the Farranfore Airport to discuss more intimate matters.

I delivered my precious passenger back home to the cruelty of a disgruntled husband that neither deserved nor appreciated her and retired to a comfortable sleep in room seven at Horans. I was glad this time they had vacancies to facilitate me for old time's sake.

A loud banging at my bedroom door at 8 am the next morning as I was packing instantly told me it wasn't a friend. Before I could move to answer the call, a big brute of a man was standing in the doorway, declaring that he and his wife were having marriage problems (with his attitude, you didn't have to wonder why).

So, this is the ruthless, ungrateful bastard who dominates a beautiful lady's life. This was the man that society in Tralee thought would be a better person for Serica to spend her life with than me. As soon as he stopped his ranting and raging, I walked over to him, looked him straight in the eye (even though he was much bigger than me) and said, 'You or anyone else won't stop me from seeing or talking to any of my friends, and Serica's one of my best friends.'

His rage soon turned to a whimper when he saw how angry I was. I had expected him to attack me considering his height and weight, and boy, was I ready to reply—I was furious. But he turned on his heel and muttered, 'Leave my wife alone,' as he rushed away.

When I calmed down, I rang Serica to be informed that he had beaten her again the previous night on her return home. I had the fear of God in me for her safety if she continued to live with that man. We discreetly met twice more before I returned to Cork to swap stories and reminisce—this assured me that she was OK.

Niall and his friends invited me to the All Ireland final and I was flattered. I saw it as another step in the right direction. I hoped neither he nor Elizabeth saw me being back in Ireland as a threat to their stable life. I only ever saw myself as a supportive father with no intention of interfering in their lives and hoped they didn't see it otherwise. I also recognised the ball was in their court and it was for them to decide if they wished to mend the relationship and if not, so be it. I would respect their wishes either way.

God must've been having a good day in heaven for again Breda, the wonderful mediator, had organised for me to meet with Mary for breakfast and a chat. Mary was most kind and courteous to me and I complimented her on the wonderful job she did in raising Niall and Elizabeth. Half an hour was plenty as we both struggled to make conversation. I was glad for her that she was comfortable with her life, I gave her a kiss on the cheek and she blushed as we parted. *Another step in the right direction,* I thought to myself.

I ran across the road in McCurtin Street to Crowleys music shop where Joe O'Herlihy who was Rory Gallagher's, and is now U2's sound genius once worked. There I bought some guitar strings to take home to Oz. I wanted to combine my Irish-bought strings with my Aussie guitar to give me a more intimate feeling for my song writing. I rang Serica and assured her I would keep in touch.

I sang some more of my own songs in Cork and surrounding pubs to sound out their quality and I was flattered to be invited to do a Sunday morning gig in Ballincollig, but I had to decline as I would be on my way back to Australia. However, the offer left a smile on my face for a while.

Aunt Mary was oozing with pride each time I visited her, forever the angel in my life. Stef and I met a few times to discuss life on the road in Ireland as a commercial traveller and we concluded that nothing had changed, only that we had gotten older and it was still a time of secrets.

Mick and I spent more than our fair share of time together before it was time for my return to Oz. Yes, he and I made up a lot of ground: old wounds were healing rapidly and we were becoming really good mates. However, the story of Liza was getting worse. She seemed to have gotten angry because I had forgiven Mick for his past indiscretions and no amount of reassurance of my love for her was of any consolation.

Returning to Australia was exciting, I felt I had spent enough quality time with everyone that I wanted to, except I could never had enough time with my old friend, Stef. I had done a lot of bridge-mending and I felt grateful to God for giving me the opportunity to do so. Breda squeezed my hand for what seemed like forever as we parted in the airport, assuring me of the enormous love she had for her only brother. I assured her I loved her equally. On the long return journey back to Oz, I felt compelled to write down all my feelings about the trip.

Helen, Jonathan and Emmett were like greyhounds out of the trap waiting for me at Tullamarine Airport, and I was welcomed back with open arms. I thought to myself, *The Queen doesn't get a welcome like this when she visits,* and I felt privileged to be home and I was grateful to Australia for the opportunity it had given me, and the lifestyle I had enjoyed. Even if I didn't like their game of footy—surely that was democracy in its full form!

Life soon returned to normal with the usual budgets of business to be met and family affairs to attend to, and soon Christmas came and went—not once, but twice. Emmett and Jonathan grew bigger and stronger and became well-adjusted young boys, and I continued to be most grateful to Australia. My second book of poetry, *Straight From the Heart,* was completed to good reviews. Easons in Ireland agreed to stock both books in their shops in Dublin and Cork. I also wrote a song called, 'Say That You Love Me' for the National Song Contest in Ireland, fulfilling one of my long-cherished ambitions.

I packed my bags and headed off again for the Emerald Isle on a different mission. Again I was travelling alone. So, as soon as I stepped on the jumbo, it was the same old story—pen and pad in the hand and lots of tear-jerking poetry flowing. I feel now that my pen sometimes writes with tears of joy and sometimes tears of sorrow, never ink.

Ireland couldn't look anything but spectacular when flying in, even in the rain. She looked so full of mystique from the sky. Dublin was my point of entry this time as I had to deliver my submission for the song contest to RTE in Donnybrook, and that's just what I did . . . after kissing the tarmac on arrival and having my customary pint of Heineken. I was humbled when I visited Easons and got the evening newspaper to see both my books on the shelf and again I was grateful to Gurranabraher for the sense of strength it gave me and to Australia for the opportunities it had given me.

I couldn't for the life of me understand what made me head for Limerick the next morning instead of Cork, but I can only assume the puppet master was again at work and directing my very thinking. Whatever the reason, I found myself standing at Marion's door in Garryowen where her father greeted me with a smile. I could only assume he didn't recognise me. But I was wrong.

'Michael, how are you?'

I was in shock. I composed myself and tried to explain that I came to apologise, to which he replied, 'No no, it was all my fault. I didn't listen.' He politely invited me in to have some tea. Of course I accepted but I was still confused. He explained to me in detail the difficult marriage Marion went through. Unlike Serica's, Marion's was more mental than physical torture. He apologised profusely for his prejudice and disbelief of the then truth. 'You no doubt know she loved you like crazy,' he said with a smile, 'and I broke her heart when I told her never to see you again. I was so wrong.'

I let him know I understood and I was glad we both got to explain our situations at that time. 'Yes, I loved her like crazy too and no, we didn't have sex. We only ever kissed and were just magic friends.'

'I know, Mike. Again, I'm sorry.'

I asked him, 'Where is she now?' and he told me, 'She's working as a waitress in a restaurant downtown. Would you like to see her?'

'Could I?'

'Of course you can,' he replied. He gave me directions and again I was grateful to God for giving me another opportunity to mend another bridge in my life.

'Can I help you?' the waitress asked.

'Could you send Marion over to me please?' I replied. I hid my face in a newspaper as she arrived to what she thought was a hungry customer except she was in for the shock of her life.

'What would you like, sir?' she leant over. I kept my head buried in the newspaper and replied, 'To spend a week in your knickers,' and before she turned to walk away I looked into her eyes.

'Oh Jesus, oh Christ,' she trembled and sat beside me with her head in her hands and tears flowing. She searched for words, her face was snow white and she was suffering shock. I apologised for not giving her warning.

'No no,' she assured me, 'Just let me think for a minute . . . this isn't true is it?' she asked. I assured her it was real.

'Oh my God, how?' she muttered.

'I've been to see your dad and he told me where to find you.'

'Oh my God, I can't believe it's you!' Again, I assured her it was real and it was me.

'You went to see my dad?'

'Yeah,' I smiled, 'And this time, no gun pointing at me, only cups of tea and lots of chat and apologising.'

'I guess we've got a lot of talking and catching up to do.'

'Don't panic. You organise a babysitter and I'll pick you up for dinner at your place at 7.30, OK?' She agreed.

I'm never late and I certainly didn't want to be late that night so I arrived at 7.15. She had obviously informed the babysitter of our past relationship and she was as excited as Marion was to see me. Marion introduced me to her two young sons whose dad who was tragically killed.

She kissed the boys lovingly and told them to be good while she and I were out for dinner. *The Two Mile Inn hasn't changed much since my last drink here in 1973,* I thought as we entered. Marion hadn't changed either. She was still a wonderful lady with a gorgeous smile and sense of calmness about her. Yes, elegance oozed out of that lady, she sure had more than an abundance of it.

We ordered drinks from the waiter and toasted our good luck to have found each other again. I was lost for an explanation when she asked, 'What made you turn up today?' All I could do was shrug my shoulders and look up to the heavens. 'It must be Him—unfinished business and bridges to mend.' Marion replied, 'Speaking of unfinished business, Mike, remember no one would ever believe we didn't have sex?' I sheepishly replied, 'Yeah, why?' She said, 'Well, we were accused of it, so now we may as well have the benefit. Finish your drink and let's put it right and bugger dinner, what do you say?'

I was flattered and we were like a couple of school kids trying but unable to open the bag of lollies. Still, we sure had fun trying in the back seat of the car. 'OK, now we can have dinner,' she said with an enormous smile. She looked radiant, not unlike Bo Derek.

I spent another day and night in Limerick catching up on lost time with Marion. We will forever until our dying days be soulmates. Again, I thanked my God for mending another bridge.

I made a quick trip to Tralee to check on Serica's situation. No change, he was still being a bastard and life was still not good to her.

I headed for Cork to attend the official release of my two books at a launch in 'Murphy Brewery Hospitality Room'. Breda—again the organiser—to my amazement had arranged for the renowned surgeon, Doctor Maurice Hickey, to come to the launch. Yeah, the very same man who used his magic skills all those years ago in St. Finbars Hospital to save my life. I was humbled and in disbelief throughout the entire event. It was a wonderful feeling to come back to your place of birth and get recognition for your craft. And, guess what? More was to come—'Say That You Love Me' made it into the National Song Contest.

The next day, I stood outside the New School in Cathedral Road and grinned. I had my satisfaction. They told me that I wouldn't amount to anything and I was tone deaf. I screamed through the railing fence, 'WHAT DO YOU SAY NOW?' I knew no one was listening, but that didn't matter. I had answered my critics in the best manner—with success.

In a strange way, I reflected as I stared at the school, maybe the most motivating thing that I ever got at that school was being told I would never amount to anything. At last, I felt different as I walked away. Another bridge was being repaired. I was also honoured by a request from the Lord Mayoress to attend City Hall to swap gifts and pleasantries.

It would have taken a very strong wind to take the smile off Aunt Mary's face as we walked from Barrett's buildings down to Mahoney's Bar in Blarney Street for her half-pint and a drop of whiskey. We sat in the corner with her lovingly looking into my eyes, and reaching down to my very soul. I asked, 'How did you know I would do it? How did you know I had the strength to get through all of this?'

She just beamed the most beautiful smile. 'Sure, aren't I your guardian angel? Of course, I knew and you will go on to even bigger and better things because you have a wonderful heart and soul inside you. Did you know that God gave special things to you when you were born? He knew you were the right person to be looking after them, he wanted you to do wonderful things in this life and you will—that's your job. You will have a huge impact on other kids from deprived backgrounds like yourself, and it won't stop there, you mark my words. Sadly, I won't be here to read your next book, but I know what you're going to write and you know what you have to write.' She squeezed my hand. 'No more secrets, OK, son? Now go out there and make a bigger name for yourself.'

She took my breath away with her comments. I found it impossible to respond with words. Slowly I walked her home and sat her in her favourite chair. Tears were still in my eyes as we parted. 'I'll be watching, I'll always be watching.' I closed her door behind me and stepped back into the world of mortals again, leaving my angel behind.

Mick and I did the occasional pub crawl and he was flattered with the attention we got and he was only too happy to tell everyone he consented on a few occasions to collaborate on some of my poems for my books. I was happy that he was happy, and proud too, for that was all I wanted and felt this bridge was truly mended.

Elizabeth finally agreed to meet with me and we spent an afternoon in the beautiful town of Cobh, the last port of call for *The Titanic* before her fatal voyage. In hindsight, perhaps it was for me also in my relationship with Liz. I explained everything to her as to why and how

I left her mum, Niall and herself. I explained about the wet beds, living with the in-laws and the fact that her mum would not leave the in-laws' house to make a home for the four of us. I guess a lot of time and a lot of prejudice with ill-intentioned stories had gotten to her and poisoned her views and I couldn't help but feel that my explanation fell on deaf ears.

It didn't offend me that that was the way it was because, who knows? She, like me, may one day come to realise that life is about tomorrow and not yesterday. And hopefully we all learn from our mistakes and move on just like I did with Mick. I was, however, grateful to at least have been given the opportunity to explain my side of the story to her and whatever way the dice comes up it will always be the same. She is my daughter and I am her dad.

Yes, God was good to me. I know that now. In fact, He was very good to me. Aunt Mary was right. Sure, not everything turned out perfectly—I didn't win the National Song Contest, even though Fran Meen and the Mean Machine did a brilliant job on the night. Even though Liza never told me so, I was sure that that night, along with the release of my books, were some of her proudest moments.

So, before I packed my bags again and headed for Oz, I reflected once more on some of the magic things that life had thrown up at me ... You have a young lad born into poverty, but life and the puppet master have other plans for him. His life is like a current stockmarket: up one minute, down the next. He soon gets a Master's degree at the University of Life on the streets of Gurranabraher. He has to go through bad times to appreciate the good times, and there are plenty of both. He knows and appreciates every time he sits at a table of fine food what others not so fortunate as him are having—perhaps sheep's head soup. He knows what it's like to sleep in a clean, dry bed with the smell of lemon all around, a stark contrast to his earlier life.

He knows poverty as if it were his second name, but he also knows everything isn't forever and reaching for the sky is not an impossible dream for people do it every day—they're called pilots! He understands life sometimes catches you by the scruff of the neck and then dumps you in a puddle of shit and, then again, you look into the eyes of a newborn baby and you see wonders. Never take it for granted, for as sure as you have it, you may lose it, so appreciate it while you have it. Always be grateful for the good things in life, for not everyone is fortunate enough to have them.

Life was good to the young man from Gurranabraher. Sure, he's had his tough times, but he's also learnt that having his own angel to believe in him was a huge motivating factor, and he's gained enormous strength from that.

He has learned the difference between success and failure is only one word—Attitude and, sadly, not a lot of that was dished out in the New School in Gurranabraher. He's also learned that losing one lung (which explains why he is not all there) at the age of seven, and being dyslexic, and not being able to read and write on leaving school should not mean one is doomed to a life of poverty. On the contrary, those things should be used as stepping-stones and not millstones. He has learned to love and be loved, he has also drunk from the fountain of bitterness. He declares it's better to have loved and lost, than to never have experienced love at all.

Yes, life is a wonderful river, always flowing, never the same, always something new around the next bend and, honestly, I wouldn't want it any other way. As with the seasons always changing, so must life. Yes, we love the sunshine but then look at the contrast in a carpet of snow, for if the rain doesn't fall we don't get roses. And so to us mortal humans we also have a constant change, that's how life must be and we can only do our best and sometimes that's not good enough, but then again it's taken men to the moon.

More importantly, we must always make sure that we give of our best to the children for, like the young man from Gurranabraher I once was, belief in me gave me enormous strength. Hopefully by me laying a period of my life out for observation, the cycle of lies can—and will—be broken, and Ireland will no longer be in a time of secrets.

There were no more tears on leaving Ireland this time, as my heart was a lot more content and a lot of bridges had been mended. Sure, I still had some more to mend, and I hoped with a little help from the puppet master, and my very own angel, over time those broken bridges would also be repaired. If not, it wouldn't be for lack of trying. From the plane I looked back at Ireland as it faded in the distance and thanked God for being so good to me as I knew I would be back again soon. In the meantime, there was a book to be written: *A Time of Secrets.*

EPILOGUE

SERICA, WELL SHE and I haven't met for almost ten years now. I believe she's in a new relationship. Some time back, she hired a private detective to monitor the brutal husband and, true to the cycle of lies, the husband was deceiving her. Justice was finally done and my heart is now at ease for her.

I sometimes wonder, 'what if?' and then again perhaps it might never have worked out for us as we would have liked it to. I'm so sorry her mum passed away before I could make peace with her.

Marion is in a new relationship also and cherishing it this time around. She still looks the picture of elegance. We still catch up occasionally for a coffee and a chat about old times and marvel at the wonders of the world. Sadly, her dad passed away soon after he and I got to reconcile. Now I understand why the puppet master guided me to Limerick that day.

Aunt Mary—my own angel on earth—returned home to heaven on January 10, 2000, and I'm just grateful that she picked me to guide through the maze called life. Yes, I talk to her regularly for I know she's always by my side and every time I get into trouble, her words are like a good kick in the arse: 'You may have been born in shit but you don't have to live in it. Now go out there and make a name for yourself.'

Thank you, my angel.

Breda found peace, finally. After many years, she came to terms with her torrid past. She nursed Mick in the final years of his life before he passed away on January 13, 1993. I'm sure the compassion she showed him helped her put the demons of the past behind her. She now spends her time doting on grandchildren and a little boy she and Tim adopted, Cian. And, as she always says, she misses her only brother and hates Australia for taking him away from her.

Stef has never changed. He's always smooth, calm and collected. He's just a wonderful giving person, still on the road, but not as often. Forever the brother I never had.

Liza passed away on January 22, 1996. I don't think she ever forgave me for forgiving Mick for his past indiscretions. We were forever at loggerheads and, to this day, it leaves a huge burden on my heart. I somehow think she carried an amount of guilt within herself for not being there for us as children and then later on she didn't know how to deal with it. Not supporting Breda in the times she needed her most wouldn't have made it any easier to come to terms with her own past. Everyone I meet tells me how she always spoke about my success and said how proud she was, but sadly, she never told me.

Clifford Davis I haven't seen for about fifteen years and have no knowledge of his whereabouts, but I do say the odd Hail Mary for his wellbeing and safety, as I've always feared for it.

Bob Dallas I haven't seen for close to 25 years. But I will always be grateful to him and his friends for the kindness they showed me when I desperately needed it.

Niall is in business for himself and is doing very well. He's married with children. We haven't caught up for some years now.

Elizabeth and I are still very much estranged.

Jonathan is now 24 and forever my best mate. He works in the technology services world and is a very talented young man.

Emmett is 20 and a wonderful musician—everything I'm not. He is also a dyslexic person, like myself. He is one of the kindest young men you'll ever meet. He's got a smile to die for and we recently co-wrote our first song and had it produced in Ireland. He aspires to one day manage the Conrad Hotel in Dublin. He works in the world of hospitality and, like Jonathan, is my best mate.

Me, well I've come a long way from my childhood days. I pinch myself every morning and thank God for the wonderful journey I've been on. Sure, I've had some tough times, but I've learned from them and used them as a springboard to a better life. The decision I made with the arrival of Jonathan and Emmett, to be their mate through thick and thin, was born out of previous experiences. And boy, did I get that right! We are inseperable—well, until they meet their respective partners.

So, I continue to learn from my mistakes.

Helen and I no longer shared the same views of our future together and so with the greatest amount of dignity, we live separate lives and have enormous respect for each other.

My first song to be recorded was by a Dublin group called, The Dublin Rogues, the song was, 'Dublin Sundays'. Since then, I have been privileged to work with many talented and famous singers and musicians. I was privileged to have one of my songs, 'Harmony', showcased by Peter Williams of The Mixtures on a visit to Australia by the then Irish Taoiseach (Prime Minister), Albert Reynolds, T.D.

I have also been privileged to sit on many boards: The Irish Australian Chamber of Commerce, and the Celtic Club, to name a few. My insertion into the music industry brought me to the presidency of The Australian Songwriters Association Inc., where I stayed for some years. And in turn, with my business partner, Alan Sherratt, that opportunity led us through the doors of the European Broadcasting Union in Geneva, via Liam Miller and RTE, to work on changing and revamping the structure of the Eurovision Song Contest (ambition fulfilled). I must admit I get enormous pleasure these days when I see young talent from non-English speaking nations getting opportunities that they would not otherwise have had if it wasn't for an Alan Sherratt from Birmingham and a Mike Bowen from Cork.

That experience, coupled with my experience on a certain board in Melbourne and an unnamed TV station that organised a worldwide-known music dance event, are earmarked to be the subject of another book, *Looking For Answers*. But before that, I have to complete my pet project—it's what my friends and family call my mad times, *The True Story of Noah and The Ark* (Noah of course being an Irishman and if anything is going to go wrong . . .).

Who said you can't take coal to Newcastle? One of my ambitions was to at least to try do something similar, and that was borne out when I brought an Australian band, The Travelling Wallabies, to do Irish music in Ireland. If you ever wondered what you can do with dreams, mine came true when The Wallabies played in front of an estimated 70,000 people on the main stage in Denny Street, at the opening of the Rose of Tralee Festival in September, 1991.

Then on Friday October 6, 2000, my dear friend and music promoter, Rob Hall, organised a special audience for me with the wonderfully talented songwriter, Jimmy Webb, who wrote 'Where's the Playground, Susie?', 'By the Time I Get to Phoenix,' and lots of other wonderful classics.

Yes, I have come a long way from having patches on the arse of my trousers. I have been privileged in so many ways: to have the foresight to grasp opportunities and work hard, to have the love and support of some magic people who helped me on my way, and I thank God for the good sense not to bear grudges and carry chips on my shoulder.

My greatest wish now is that people will find something good in my life to complement theirs and, by opening up my life warts and all, as I have done here, we may all live a more open, honest life. I want the time of secrets to be no more, for our children's sake. I am who I am

... nothing more, nothing less and I'll wear the name Michael Bowen until the end of my days like a badge of honour, as Aunt Mary would wish. And I ask that you don't dislike me for what I'm not, but like me for what I am.